1.00

gifts from the garden

gifts from the garden

By SUZANNE JAMES

Drawings by Elsa

Hearthside Press   •   Incorporated
Publishers   •   New York

to steve

TABLE OF CONTENTS

1

the art of giving

This book was written to help you see your garden with a fresh viewpoint: as a source of materials for interesting gifts and an introduction to unusual crafts, most of them easily learned. Whatever the size of the available space—a tiny backyard or even a window box indoors—it can be useful and productive in making gifts that symbolize the wish to share something you love with someone you love.

Giving is a habit born of thoughtfulness. It needs neither occasion nor holiday to function; in fact, the element of surprise makes an unexpected token doubly appreciated. The gardener whose visitors rarely leave empty-handed—they carry home a jar of raspberry preserves, a potted African violet, a flowering branch, crisp lettuce leaves and sunwarmed tomatoes for an evening salad—has learned the fine habit of giving. He reaps a fine harvest too—the personal satisfactions that come from considering others, and the pleasure of giving without thought of price.

One of the nicest aspects of the gift you make yourself is the joy it brings to those who receive it. In this age of mass-production, is there anyone who does not value the present made at home, with its implied "one-of-a-kind" label?

THE TECHNIQUE OF GIVING

Knowing your friends' likes and dislikes, and helping to fill their needs, is probably the ultimate in the art of giving. Since trusting to memory is a chancy business, it is sensible to use a card file. Here you can record preferences which your friends may have mentioned casually, comments about color schemes, notes about favorite foods and flowers, and important dates—all this in anticipation of the occasion for which you may wish to send a corsage, a flower arrangement, or a potted plant.

Keep all your wrappings, twine, card file, mailing equipment and stamps in one place. If possible make a work center with space and tools for handling flowers, wrapping gifts, storing dried materials, and perhaps propagating plants. With everything so conveniently at hand, giving will be simpler, more pleasant, and therefore more frequent.

Happily, many different skills and hobbies can be combined with gardening to produce imaginative and worthwhile gifts. Here are suggestions for utilizing hobbies of your own and other members of the family:

Ceramics, Carpentry, Mosaics: Design and make containers for house plants. Prepare frames for flower pictures. Build a window box to hold potted plants. Construct your special work area.

Rockhounding, Driftwood Hunting: Save natural treasures to use as part of bonsai and in minature landscapes. Rocks and wood conceal mechanics which hold flowers in arrangements.

Candlemaking and Woodcarving: Garden fragrancies can be incorporated into the candles, a delight to the sense of smell. Carve miniature accessories for miniature landscapes.

Sketching: Draw your own greeting cards from flowers, sketch your flower arrangements before you make them, outline your design for a seed mosaic.

Photography: Keep a picture record of your garden. Photograph arrangements and ambitious seed mosaics before you give them away. Present pictures of your flowers in color, attractively framed. Make photograms (see index).

A CALENDAR FOR GIVING

In many of us, the desire for giving is often suppressed because time, money or materials are lacking. Your garden, however, can be a treasury from which to withdraw gifts as you need them. With the following guide, you can plan and give presents all year around.

January: Birthday flowers—snowdrop, carnation. Give leis, friendship branches, heather as symbols of good luck. Gilded dried material will please the New Year hostess. Send a flowering plant to brighten a winter-weary friend.

February: Birthday flower—primrose. Send a potted flowering bulb to your Valentine. The man in your life enjoys them, although he rarely thinks of buying them for himself. Send a corsage to the children's teacher. Make heart-shaped sachets and seed mosaics. For Washington's Birthday, hang bright red cherries, real or artificial, from a driftwood branch stuck into styrofoam in a pot.

March: Birthday flower—violet or jonquil.
The luck of the Irish to him who gets a packet of bells-of-Ireland seed on March 17! Give with these instructions—"Sow the seed in early spring. The plants will bloom (to 3 feet high) before summer. Next spring the ripe seed which falls to the ground will come up by itself. The bracts are long lasting even when cut for flower arrangements. They dry well and can be sprayed for Christmas decorations. The seed which is inside the bell can be given to another lucky Irishman next St. Patrick's Day."

To celebrate the first day of spring, send forced branches of forsythia, quince or other flowering shrub on March 21. Pot up a few lily-of-the-valley pips to bloom indoors. Divide mums, pot them for Fall gifts.

April: Birthday flower—lily or sweetpea. Send baskets filled with daffodils, mimosa, calla lilies or pussy willows for Easter. Make calla lilly garnishes for the Easter hostess (see index). A colonial bouquet of violets is an antidote for the rainy month. Start seed propagation projects for the children home for Eastern vacation.

May: Birthday flower—lily-of-the-valley. Hang a May Day basket on a neighbor's door and revive a charming custom! Filled with geraniums or maybe plants for a rockery or herb garden, it will bring back heartwarming memories.

For Mother's Day, the second Sunday of the month, send her favorite flowers. Or make an arrangement which includes something for her favorite hobby—maybe a bit of needlepoint, or a new casserole? What about a few potted African violets or geraniums?

Save lots of time for planting! Don't forget gourds.

June: Birthday flower—rose.

For showers and weddings, give food gifts, seed panels, plaques of dried seed pods. One woman I know specializes in arranging flowers from her garden for simple home weddings—a real gift for the bride and her family. Driftwood planters, a bonsai or miniature garden would be excellent too. Make corsages for the shower guests.

For graduation, the wise cone owl (see index) would be fun to get. Also give a corsage for the prom girl.

For Father, the third Sunday, why not make a flat of well grown seedlings, or send a big green plant to decorate his office?

Tie a corsage of the birthday flowers (this month, roses) to your birthday package.

July: Birthday flower—larkspur.

For Independence Day, July 4, send red and white carnations and purple-blue iris. Red geraniums, white Queen Anne's lace, and blue cornflowers are another possibility. This is a big month for new babies—send a toy cradle filled with herbs as a symbol of good luck.

August: Birthday flower—gladiolus.

Tie a small corsage to the box supper prepared for a house guest. A basket filled with home-grown tomatoes and other vegetables, and lots of mint (roots, soil and all wrapped in aluminum foil) makes a pretty "welcome home" for a friend. Carry a large branch of foliage in a jar filled with glycerine to the winner of the golf tournament—he'll think you're cool! Time to start some canning, preserving, freezing!

September: Birthday flower—aster. Send teacher a pomander ball made with an apple instead of an orange (see index). For friends who are moving, start a garden of cuttings from your own plants. A miniature garden or bonsai, plaques made from seeds, pine cones for the fireplace, or a welcome mat with fragrant herbs, are unusual. A good month to propagate English ivy for making an Ivy Tree, Christmas wreath, etc. Save seeds for mosaics and three-dimensional plaques. Order bulbs for indoor bloom. Select trees for bonsai. Glycerine branches.

October: Birthday flower—dahlia or calendula.

Fill grinning pumpkins with autumn leaves. Jack o'lanterns filled with soil and chrysanthemums, and candied apples-on-a-stick for trick-or-treat bell ringers are good projects for this month.

November: Birthday flower—chrysanthemum.

Send a cornucopia filled with fruit. Make charm strings from shocks of grain, corn, squash, gourds, zucchini and peppers for friends to hang on their front door. Armloads of mums will delight the Thanksgiving hostess (fourth Thursday in November). A good month for making all kinds of gifts from dried materials. Collect weathered wood too.

December: Birthday flower—holly or narcissus.

For Christmas, send evergreens and holly, wreaths, garlands and swags. Corsages, sachets, rose jars, wax flowers—just about everything in this book! Make lots of seed and nut corsages for decorating gift packages.

GIFTS TO THE COMMUNITY

In Monterey, California, we celebrate an annual event called Cutting Day. Home gardeners, nurserymen and the park and recreation departments bring extra cuttings to share with friends and neighbors, and many a youngster has developed a love for gardening which stems from planting one of these free cuttings. Can you imagine a better gift to your community than a Cutting Day which brings it so much pleasure and beauty? Why not suggest that your garden club sponsor such an event?

If you are trying to raise money for an organization, consider having a Fragrance Booth at the next bazaar, especially if held around Christmas time. Potpourris, lotions, sachets, pomander balls, soap, perfumed ink, and sweet-smelling stuffed dolls can be prepared ahead by a committee following the directions in Chapter 6. Such a booth might also include fragrant cut flowers and corsages for sale, with demonstrations to show how the various items are made.

Other good gifts would include labeled cuttings, dried herbs, wax flowers, herb jellies, mobiles, and flowers preserved in plastic.

A gift of your time is priceless. Perhaps you can set aside an hour or two each week for teaching cub scouts, campfire girls or senior citizens how to propagate plants. A neighbor working her first garden would welcome your advice and help too. There is therapy in horticulture for people who are in an institution, if those of us who are lucky will give a gift of time.

2

flower arrangements, corsages and novelties

Have you ever known a woman whose face did not light up at a gift of flowers? It seems to me the most universally accepted manner of expressing sentiment for others. The gift need not be lavish: a few garden rosebuds in a glass jar remind a friend that she is loved and remembered, which is, after all, the point of most presents.

Undeniably, however, not all floral giving can be so casual. For those women we know rather formally, and for many occasions, even with close friends, thought must be given to design. For instance, flowers brought to a party should be arranged beforehand, otherwise the hostess feels compelled to do so, however busy she may be with last-minute details. Also, when the garden offers little to cut—perhaps five daffodils or a handful of mums—a line arrangement conceals the dearth of material. Flowers carried to a sickroom should always be ready to set on a table; they have more lasting interest for the patient if they are arranged with some design plan. Finally, I think that dried flowers are always more effective when made into an arrangement before they are presented.

Many books have been written about arranging flowers—Hearthside Press alone has published thirty-one, all of them in print. Obviously, an art which deserves so much literature is complex. In these pages, we can give only a few basic facts. I hope they will help you with your first design, and possibly save you the embarrassment of presenting an arrangement which falls apart in transportation because you do not know some of the mechanical facts of floral design.

DESIGNING YOUR FIRST ARRANGEMENT, Fig. 1

Learning to arrange flowers is similar to learning to cook. It is much easier at first if you follow a recipe. When you have mastered the basics, you can improvise, add or substitute as you wish. In fact, the more expert you become, the more likely you are to break the "rules." One rule, however, always will apply: *all flowers and foliage must be conditioned first.*

A) Manipulate floral clay into a roll ½-inch in diameter. Place clay all around the pinholder and press into position in container. Be sure pinholder and container are thoroughly dry first. If you are using plastic foam to hold flowers, soak it in water before you insert the flowers.

B) The longest branch or flower should be about 2½ times the height or width of the container, whichever dimension is larger. Make your outline or skeleton with spiky, thin flowers or foliage.

C) Fill in with medium size flowers. The palest, smallest flowers are generally the ones furthest from the focal point. The eye is carried to the focal point with successively larger and brighter flowers or foliage.

D) The stems of flowers and foliage seem to meet at one point in the container, usually at the rim.

E) The most colorful, unusual and largest blossom is placed where all stems meet; this becomes the focal point.

The pinholder or plastic foam used to hold the flowers must never be evident.

Some arrangements use only one kind of flowers, others a variety, but all stems are cut to different lengths. In a symmetrical design, two sides are the same, so two stems are cut to each different length.

Be sure the flower arrangement will suit its setting. The woman whose home is done in white and gold, with accents of orange, is unlikely to enthuse over a gift of pink and magenta flowers. A file to record such preferences makes good sense.

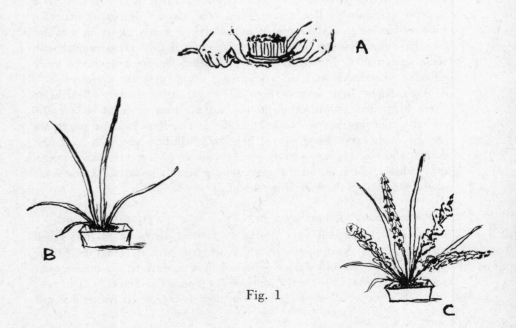

Fig. 1

D

E

Pinholders or plastic foam?

Pinholders are the best mechanical aids for holding flowers in place. They pierce the stems, giving flowers a chance to breathe and thus preserving their life. However, plastic foam—sold under such trade names as Oasis, non-spillable water, Sno-Pak, and Hydrofoam—is preferred by most florists for several reasons: arrangements in pinholders take more time, pinholders are more expensive than foam, and arrangements in foam can be transported more easily since water cannot spill. Arrangers planning gifts have similar problems and will find plastic foam useful.

Containers and Accessories

When cost is not a consideration choosing a container offers little problem. Cut glass bowls, a brass chafing dish, attractive casseroles, silver serving bowls, crystal pitchers and a wide variety of other materials—in addition of course to vases planned for that purpose—can hold flowers. Essentially, the point to remember is that they should be of a color, shape and texture that does not compete with the flowers.

At times, however, for economy and expediency, you may need improvised containers. Large sea shells, driftwood, and vegetables and fruits, which have the added advantage of keeping flowers moist, are among the

Plate 1 An autumn gift displays the bounty from a flower and vegetable garden. Variegated privet, yellow celosia, yellow goldenrod, pyracantha berries, marigolds in shades of yellow through orange with deeper orange zinnias, orange squash, zucchini squash and peppers are arranged in a pumpkin.

Arranged by Mrs. George Goldson   (Photo Sevecke)

Fig. 2

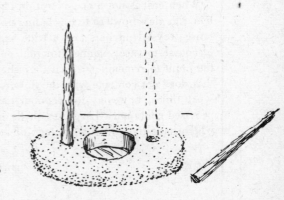

Fig. 3

possibilities. One charming gift to a barbecue hostess was a centerpiece of short-stemmed flowers arranged in plastic foam in a loaf of French bread which had been hollowed out and lined with aluminum foil. Perfume and beverage bottles are usually well designed and can become floral vases.

The containers in Plate 1 and 2 are inexpensive, yet either arrangement would suit even the most sophisticated of hostesses. Plate 1 uses a pumpkin, and Plate 2 a tuna-fish can inserted into a styrofoam block. The procedures for making them are shown in Figures 2 and 3. Fig. 2 shows the order in which the plant material is inserted in plastic foam which was first soaked in water.

Plate 2 Any hostess would welcome a centerpiece arrangement. This features pink snap-dragons and white chrysanthemums with pittosporum and arborvitae.
Arranged by Mrs. George Goldson   (*Photo H. R. Glinten Kamp*)

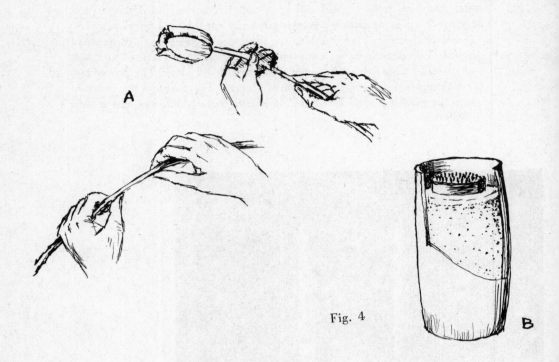

Fig. 4

TRICKS WITH PLANT MATERIAL, Fig. 4

A) To bend plants such as wisteria, Scotch broom, tulips, pussy willows etc. to desired curves, gently manipulate stems to shape you want. Soaking them in a pail of warm water first makes the stems more pliable. Some stems may also be wired to shape, see technique under Corsages.

B) Vase too tall? Fill most of it with sand, crumpled newspaper or tissue. Set a tuna fish can filled with soaked foam or a cup pinholder on top to hold flowers.

C) Stems too short? Insert them into a larger hollow stem or tie to a florist pick or toothpick to lengthen.

D) Neck of vase too wide? Fill it with crushed chicken wire.

CUTTING AND CONDITIONING FLOWERS

To a novice, conditioning flowers seems to be an unnecessary and time-consuming procedure, but it is here that the ultimate success of your arrangement or corsage begins. Conditioning flowers makes it possible for them to retain more moisture, and lessens the shock of their removal from the parent plant. They last much longer than otherwise, and endurance is a big factor in giving flowers.

Procedure:

1. Pick flowers early in the morning or in the evening when they have most moisture. Buds and flowers just coming out of the bud stage will last longer than those that are fully opened. Flowers should be crisp to the touch rather than soft.

2. Use only a very sharp knife or garden shears. Cut stems on the slant to give a greater area for soaking up moisture. Later, if necessary to secure them into pinholders, you can make a straight cut. Strip off unnecessary foliage. Foliage below the water line will decay.

3. Carry with you to the garden a pail of tepid water in which you should immediately put the cut flowers. Lukewarm water is absorbed more quickly than cold. Do not crowd the flowers in the pail either while collecting or hardening them. After the stems have been treated, soak the flowers in a cool, dark, draft-free place for a few hours or overnight.

STEM TREATMENT FOR BETTER WATER INTAKE

Soft stems of annuals, etc.: Make a short cut in the center of the base of the stem.

Bulbous stems such as daffodils, etc.: Press juice from the bottom of stem.

Hollow stems of delphiniums, dahlias, hollyhocks, etc. Dip the bottom of the stem into boiling water, or over flame, for a few seconds to sear stem. Protect flowers from steam by making a newspaper collar first.

Woody stems of perennials and shrubs such as chrysanthemums, stocks, heather, and rhododendron, etc. Crush outer skin lightly with a hammer.

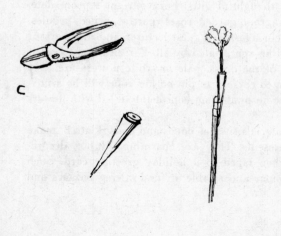

C

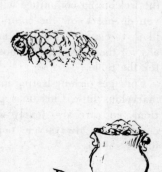

D

Roses. Sandpaper stems to remove thorns, then strip off about two inches of the outer bark from the end of stem.

Fragrant flowers. Cover them with a hood of cellophane or wax paper. Remove just before giving present. Flowers will retain fragrance.

ARRANGING DRIED FLOWERS

Flowers dried or preserved according to the directions in Chapter 3 need special handling. Such flower arrangements are highly valued because they last so long; they are especially nice gifts for those who do not have a garden of their own. Dried arrangements may be made ahead of time and put into a stockpile of gifts. A few pointers:

1. To restore freshness to a dried arrangement, fill a small bathroom with steam (turn on hot water full force) and let arrangement steam for about 15 minutes.

2. Dried stems break more easily than fresh ones. With floral tape, tie short or broken stems to long stems or to florist sticks.

3. Driftwood (see Chapter 3) has just the right weathered, soft quality to go with dried flowers. Use as a container or accessory.

4. If you do not have a cutting garden, wildlings such as pearly everlasting, goldenrod, strawflowers, cattails, Joe-Pye-Weed, Queen Anne's lace, and sumac (best in the Fall), also many wild seed pods and grasses, all dry beautifully.

CORSAGES AS GIFTS

The word corsage usually produces an image of roses, orchids or gardenias, but our gardens are filled with enchanting possibilities: violets, carnations, camellias, chrysanthemums, asters, daisies, marigolds, cornflowers, dwarf zinnias, scabiosa, calendulas, azaleas, tuberous begonias, and peonies. For foliage, camellia, geranium, gardenia, magnolia, holly, ivy, even pachysandra. Dried materials and succulents are also ideal.

Corsages are personal and thoughtful gifts. For your son's prom date, make a delicate one from fragrant garden roses, partly opened peonies, azaleas, or garden pinks. A corsage for a guest lecturer and members of the welcoming committee will be appreciated by all. For either purpose, if you do not know the colors of the dress, pale or white flowers are least likely to clash. A sweetly scented corsage to pin on her robe will be a novelty for the new mother, whose hospital room is probably filled with flowers for the table.

Corsages of long-lasting materials such as cones and pods, Plate 3, make marvelous little Christmas presents. They are charming gift-box decorations, and are also lovely when taped to a holiday greeting card. Such corsages are always very popular and salable at fund-raising bazaars and flower shows.

MAKING YOUR FIRST CORSAGE

There are many different techniques, but the ones given below are basic. You will need the supplies shown in Plate 4. First condition flowers for several hours according to the procedure on page 18.

A. Cut off all but one inch of the natural stems.

B. Wire flowers following one of the methods given below. Touch petals as little as possible when you work.

C. Wind floral tape (one-half-inch wide) around stem to conceal mechanics. Do not overlap tape more than necessary or its gets lumpy. Hold flower with left hand, twirling it between thumb and forefinger as you wrap. Stretch tape slightly as you work.

Plate 3   Long-lasting corsages have many uses and are a "must" for the gift giver's storehouse. These are made with cones, seed pods, and nuts with some of the cones cut in half to produce a flat, flower-like effect.
Designed by Mrs. H. W. Van Hoy

(Photo Jeannette Grossman)

Green tape is best for fresh flowers, brown tape for dried flowers, and white tape for bridal corsages.

D. Assemble the corsage (see Fig. 6).

E. If you want a bow, make several loops of ribbon. Wire middle to make bow. Fasten bow to ends of corsage with wire. Trim ribbon ends as shown in Fig. 24.

F. If corsage is made of fresh plant material, sprinkle with water or clear floral spray and put into plastic bag immediately. Fill bag with air by blowing into it, then fold over bottom to seal. Fasten with a corsage pin or two and refrigerate until you are ready to give corsage. A corsage box adds to the niceties.

THE BASIC TECHNIQUES OF WIRING AND TAPING, Fig. 5

Wiring and taping are the basic skills of corsage making. Their primary purpose is to provide an artificial stem which will be stronger, longer, and more flexible than the natural one.

The wire you use depends on the weight of the flower—the lower the number, the heavier it is; thus, you use number 22 for a heavy flower such as a gardenia, and number 30 and 32 for small flowers and for binding the flowers together. However, number 26 wire is a good, all-purpose size.

There are *three basic types of wiring* to use depending on the type of

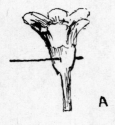
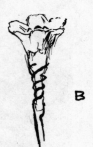

Fig. 5

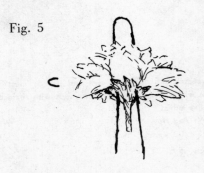

flower: piercing, hairpin and hook wiring. With any of the methods, cut off most of the natural stem, leaving only one inch.

Piercing method: Pierce the calyx of the flower at a right angle, and pull the wire through to about ⅓ of its length (A). Wrap the longer wire around the calyx and bring it down parallel to the stem, (B).

Hairpin Wiring method: Bend wire into hairpin shape with both ends even (C). Push it through the flower or leaf from the top, keeping the wire parallel to the stem; twist one wire around stem and other wire (D). This method may also be used for wiring leaves and heavy materials.

Hook method: For buds as well as bell-type and face flowers such as fuchsias and zinnias. Bend one end of the wire into a tiny hook and push the straight end of the wire down into the flower parallel to the stem (E). Wrap the wire around the stem (F).

Once wired your flower and leaf will need to be *taped* (G) not only to give the appearance of a natural stem, but also to hide the wire and protect the clothing. Use ½-inch stemming tape such as Floratape which is self-adhering. Tape as high as possible around the base of the flower and wrap tape tightly around the stem. Hold the flower with the left hand, twirling it between the thumb and the forefinger as you wrap tape down the wire stem.

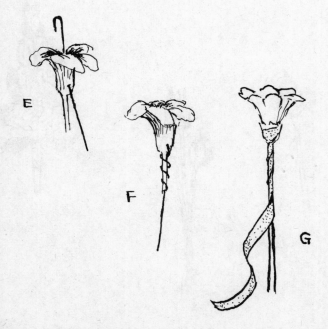

E

F

G

Plate 4   The basic supplies for corsage making are florist tape, wire, ribbon, corsage pins, and a supply of plants; in this case, nuts, cones and seed pods are used to make attractive long-lasting corsages. Nuts and pods may be brushed with clear shellac and dried before holes are bored for wiring.   *(Photo Jeannette Grossman)*

Fig. 6

ASSEMBLING THE CORSAGE, Fig. 6

There are two major types of corsage assembly:

The One-Way Corsage:

This is also known as the natural style corsage, because you wear it the way flowers grow, with the stems down.

An uneven number of flowers makes a more interesting arrangement. The flowers may be in different stages of development, or use all buds, or all fully open blossoms. You may also use either one kind of flower only, or a variety of flowers.

Begin by wiring and taping each flower, then arranging the flowers in an attractive design. If you are using flowers in different transitional stages, start with the smallest flower for the top of the corsage, working down to the largest flower at the bottom of the corsage.

Wrap stems around each other as you assemble. Use fine wire number 30 to tightly secure stems. If you add a bow, nestle it in between the flowers for a more integrated look. Bend stem into graceful curve.

The *nosegay* is a form of the one-way corsage. Make this with small, preferably fragrant flowers, either mixed or of one color. Wire and tape each flower.

Arrange the flowers attractively in your hand, and use fine wire to hold them together.

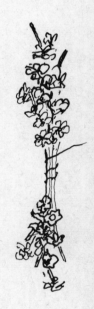

Plate 5   English ivy from the garden and a red ribbon bow make an attractive Christmas wreath. Simply bend a wire coat hanger into a circle, wind ivy around, and fasten with florists wire.   *(Photo Jeannette Grossman)*

The Two-Way Corsage

Both ends of this corsage are the same. Use all small flowers such as bouvardia or violets, or use small flowers on the ends with larger blossoms in the center.

Start with the two smallest blossoms on the ends, wiring their stems together in the center. The placement of these blossoms will determine the size of the corsage. Alternate flowers on each end, wiring each time until the corsage is finished. Trim wire, and cover with tape. Trim taped stems unevenly.

One good way to help you learn more about corsage-making is to take a ready-made corsage carefully apart, noting how it is assembled, wired, and taped and the placement of its bow; then reassemble it yourself.

MAKING FLORAL NOVELTIES

Clever and imaginative decorations can be made from flowers and other plant materials. A gift clearly marked "Please Open *Before* Christmas," comes as a welcome surprise in the busy days before the holidays. English ivy—what would we do without this versatile vine?—makes an attractive holiday wreath, Plate 5. Simply bend a wire coat hanger into a circle, wind well conditioned ivy around it, and fasten with florists wire. Fresh or waxed fruit or flowers, dried and gilded artichokes, pine cones, seed pods and berries, gourds, pomander balls and wood roses all may be wired to the wreath.

Great bundles of pine branches or holly to use for decoration, are particularly appreciated by friends in parts of the country where such material is not readily available.

You can make it a white Christmas for friends with a can of white poster paint and a medium size brush (Plate 6). A small watercolor brush is handy for reaching into small areas. Spread newspapers on your work table to catch dripping paint and place painted evergreens in a needlepoint holder to dry. When dry, arrange in Oasis or in pin holder.

Plate 6   An exciting novelty for your friends and an enchanting gift for the home of the holiday bride. A white Christmas arrangement.   *(Photo Jeannette Grossman)*

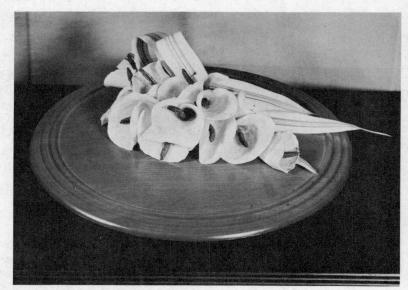

Plate 7 A spray of calla lilies "homemade" from rutabaga slices makes an amusing table
decoration. Make one for an open meeting of the garden club or for an afternoon party. For
a variation, make white callas from thin slices of turnips with stamens of carrot sticks.
Arranged by Mrs. H. Jefferson Davis (Photo B. E. Johnson)

"Home made" flowers are sure to inspire lots of conversation! In Plate
7, an effective spray of yellow "calla lilies" is fashioned from thin slices
of rutabaga softened first in hot water. Each slice is overlapped at one
end, and secured with a pin around blossoms from a pine tree. As the
flowers are made, put them in ice water to retain their crispness. Leave
them until ready to use in the spray, then attach them to a needlepoint
holder and frame them with "bows" of ribbon cane grass.

Lilies made from white turnip slices with stamens of carrot sticks would
make a piquant gift for the Easter hostess to use as a garnish.

The "magnolia" blossoms by the same arranger (Plate 8) are made by
taping "blossoms" in three stages of development onto a wisteria vine ten-
dril. As each corn shuck is removed from the ear of corn, it should be
dampened slightly to counteract the brittleness. The end of the shuck that
has been attached to the ear will have a natural curve, simulating a magnolia petal. Each shuck is shaped to size and wrapped with florist wire.
The center cedar cone is wired and the small "petals" wired together
around it. Then the outer petals are wired around the center petals. The
finished blossom is attached to the branch by tape. Spray the corn shuck
blossoms with floral paint to any desired color and give to a lady who
enjoys the unusual.

A topiary tree has infinite possibilities for giving. I have seen them used
in pairs for buffet decoration, and singly to decorate small party tables.
If planned as centerpiece gifts, the hostess should be told in advance to
expect them, of course.

Plate 8   Delight a lady who has a taste for the unusual with magnolia blossoms fashioned from corn shucks. The blossoms may be sprayed with floral paint and will prove to be a real conversation piece.
Arranged by Mrs. H. Jefferson Davis   *(Photo B. E. Johnson)*

To make the topiary tree in Plate 9, cover a round curtain rod with green floral tape. Insert it into styrofoam inside a container—this one is a plastic cup. Pour particles of colored glass or pebbles around the styrofoam until the cup is filled. At the top of the rod, secure a half-brick of Oasis which has been soaked in water. Cover Oasis with chicken wire and fill with clippings from boxwood. Add garden blossoms such as azaleas, dianthus, daisies, bachelor buttons, phlox, and miniature or floribunda roses; all plant material should be well conditioned first. A variation of this tree is shown in Plate 50.

Plate 9 A topiary tree offers many possibilities for gift giving. This one features boxwood, azalea and dianthus blossoms. Other blossoms from your garden that you might use are daisies, bachelor buttons, phlox, and miniature or floribunda roses.
Arranged by Mrs. H. Jefferson Davis   *(Photo B. E. Johnson)*

Celebrations for graduation, sweet sixteen, Mother's Day, ladies luncheons, installation of club officers, etc. are made festive with table favors, Fig. 7. A place card holder (A) is made from one flower surrounded by several small leaves. Using the hook method, wire and tape the central flower or foliage spray making a 3″ stem. Wire and tape the leaves to fit around the central flower or spray. Allow about 3 or 4 leaves for each corsage. Wire flowers and leaves together in a corsage. Tape. Bend stem up and insert a place card. A Colonial bouquet (see procedure below) surrounded by a paper doily or nylon ruffle, (B), can be inserted into a tiny pot holding styrofoam and filled with colorful pebbles. Write the guest's name on the pot with "marks on anything" ink. Bouquets of this type are charming around a birthday cake.

Flowers to use: Pompom asters, camellias, carnations, cornflowers, pinks, zinnias, roses—any flower of moderate lasting quality can be used. Succulents such as hens-and-chicken or sedum can become take-home gifts which guests can propagate. Children especially will be thrilled if told that their party favor can be potted up in soil. Fragile flowers can be inserted into small orchid vials to keep fresh, the vial covered with leaves and place card. Single sprays of andromeda or laurel foliage can substitute for the face flowers.

Leaves: Around the central flower, English ivy, pachysandra, geranium, coral-bell or honeysuckle foliage can all be used. Leaves such as rhododendron or maple which are too large can be cut down with a scissors.

Colonial Bouquets

The flowers that you use for these small, charming circular arrangements may be all of a kind and color, or use a colorful center flower surrounded by circles of smaller flowers. Each circle may have a different kind of flower and color.

Wire all the flowers separately; wire and tape the center flower to make a 3″ stem. Place the center flower slightly higher than the circles of flowers in order to avoid a flat look. Bind all flowers to center stem tightly with fine wire. To finish the bouquet, encircle it with a paper doily, a tulle frill, geranium or ivy leaves, or use the plastic bouquet holder sold by floral supply houses. The stem should be taped to conceal the wiring.

How to Make a Flower Ball

You may use either a base of wet sphagnum moss or floral foam to make a flower ball. Hairpin wire (see page 24) into this base such flowers as daisies, carnations, or small chrysanthemums. Wire a ribbon to the top of the flower ball for a sweet sixteen to wear on her wrist (Fig. 7C).

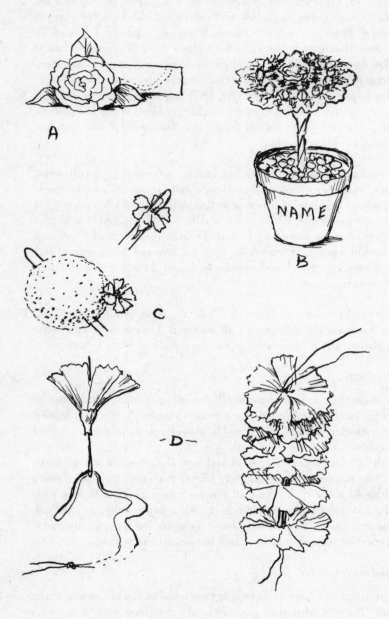

Fig. 7

A Hawaiian lei

If your garden has a plentiful supply of carnations, cornflowers, gardenias, hibiscus, zinnias, violets, or chrysanthemums, make leis (Fig. 7D) for party favors, or for a special gift for someone about to undertake a new venture.

Since leis are usually about three feet long, thread a needle with a double thread of dental floss (or a no. 40 thread) about 50 inches long. Once you have cut the stem off close to the base of the flower, you may thread the flowers either through the center or from side to side. To make the lei appear heavier, use separators of beads, knots, or small pieces of straws between the flowers.

3

gifts from long-lasting
plant materials

To the "seeing eye" of a creative gardener, there are many useful and unusual materials in nature. Seeds, cones, pods, grasses, weeds, gourds, fruits and vegetables, weathered wood and dried branches, even lichen found on tree barks (Plate 10), dry easily and can be made into gifts that last for years. Many flowers of seeming fragility can also be preserved by drying and waxing.

HOW TO DRY FLOWERS AND LEAVES
Dehydration

Cover the bottom of a low container or box with one or two inches of straight builder's sand or powdered borax (Figure 8A). A combination is also good—one part sand to two parts borax.

Place your flowers, well-spaced, face down in the mixture. Cover by sifting more of the sand—or sand and borax mixture—over them. Dry only one layer of flowers at a time. Dehydrating time varies according to the flowers and the heat of the area where the box is placed. On top of a radiator, furnace, or clothes dryer, dehydration will be accomplished in about a week; in an attic or other moderately warm dry place, it may take as long as a month.

For a speedy method, use a pyrex dish for the container, and plain builder's sand. Arrange the flowers as usual and cover with half an inch or so of sand. Place the pyrex in a very slow oven for about 10 hours. A warming well heated by a pilot light, such as some ovens have, will be just the right temperature. The flowers have a tendency to dry brown when oven-baked; with some of the chrysanthemums or other flowers in earthy colors, this is no disadvantage.

Flowers that dry especially well by dehydration are asters, carnations, daffodils, dahlias, delphiniums, dogwood, everlastings, fuchsias, geraniums, heather, irises, marigolds, pansies, violas and zinnias.

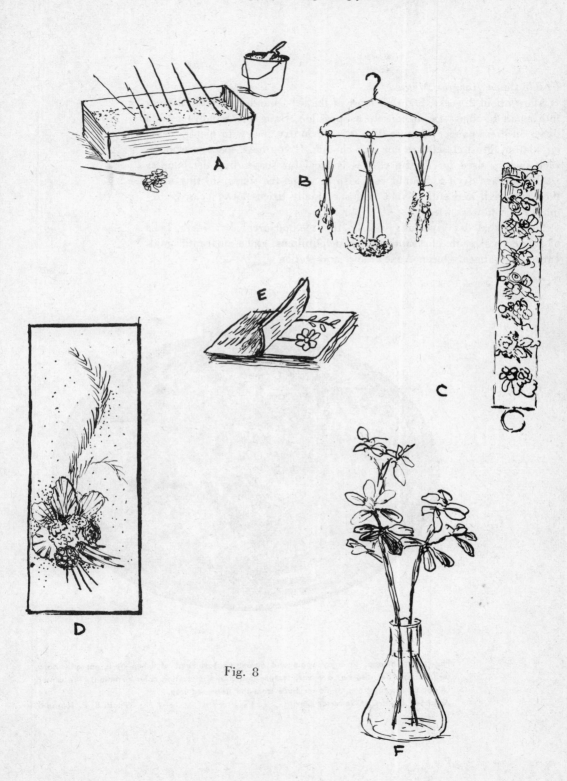

Fig. 8

Upside-Down Hanging Method

Allow about 2 weeks. Strip off most of the leaves and gather the flowers into small bundles; tie as loosely as possible. Hang the bundles upside down on dress hanger (Figure 8B) in a warm dry spot with plenty of air circulation. Most closets are not airy enough. If you have space, a wooden rack such as used for drying clothes is ideal for suspending the bundles while they are drying. Should you wish to shape the stems, do this while they are fresh and still pliable. Stems of many dried flowers can be removed and flowers wired.

Flowers that dry especially well by this method are babysbreath, bells of Ireland, coxcomb, chrysanthemums, delphiniums, globe amaranth, goldenrod, hydrangea, Queen Anne's lace, and statice.

Plate 10   Corsages to enjoy again and again are fashioned of lichen. It is not only hard and durable but also has a velvety texture and shows interesting color variations. The center cluster of the rosette is of flower buds from the dogwood tree.
Arranged by Mrs. H. Jefferson Davis

(Photo B. E. Johnson)

Plate 11   An elegant arrangement of dried and pressed plant materials makes an appropriate housewarming gift.   *Arranged by Mrs. Louis H. Amer*

Dried flowers are, of course, very useful in flower arrangements (Plate 11). The technique for assembling dried arrangements is given in Chapter 2. Plate 12 illustrates a versatile design with dried material. Four holes in the back of the plaque permit it to be hung vertically or horizontally. It may also be used as a tray.

In making gifts from dried flowers, many different procedures are possible. The dried flowers or seed pods may be sewed, wired or glued onto a background. Fabric, wood, cardboard or copper mesh are appropriate.

Fig. 8C illustrates a handsome bell pull, made by Mrs. William G. Wheeler of Roslyn Heights, N.Y. An Oriental fabric about 8" x 38" is folded in half, and sewed lengthwise with a long strip of cardboard between to add body. Gilded dried flowers and seed pods, wired into corsages, are then sewed to the silk. A brass ring at the bottom, and two tiny rings for hanging at the top, complete a lovely gift which has the look of a costly antique.

Plate 12 A versatile gift that may be used either as a wall plaque or a centerpiece tray. A small square of green styrofoam has been anchored with clay to the beige plaque. It holds glycerinized barberry for the outline material, miniature red zinnias with an orange cast, small Unwin hybrid dahlias in orange with a few red markings, and neutral green dahlia calyxes.

Arranged by Mrs. D. E. VanFleet

Plate 13   This golden ornamental tree makes an impressive gift. The understructure for the tree is a dowel with a stand and hardware cloth. Cones, seed pods, dried flowers, leaves, and small artificial fruit are individually wired and inserted into the frame. When the surface is covered, the complete tree is sprayed.   *Designed by Mrs. John L. Kestel*

In the home of Mrs. George Anders, two much-admired plaques (Fig. 8D) dominate the living room. Gifts of Mrs. George Goldson of Woodmere, New York, they are made from ordinary pieces of copper screening, 18″ wide and 5′ high, which have been framed in black bamboo. Dried cycas palm, cut palmettos, lotus pods, and cut pine cones have been wired to the screening wtih heavy wire which does not show. The muted greens and browns of the plant material, against the copper mesh background, hanging on pale beige walls, make a striking color harmony.

A golden ornamental tree (Plate 13) is a handsome Christmas gift, equally suitable for a golden wedding. To make it, cut hardware cloth to 12x12x17 inches. Sew the two 12-inch sides together to form a cone. Fill it with excelsior, stuff green felt over the bottom and make a hole in the center for a dowel 14 inches long x ½ inch in diameter (an old broomstick would do). Glue the dowel to a base 4 inches in diameter. Sharpen the other end and insert through hole in felt, push through excelsior to top of tree.

Wire each cone, seed pod, dried flower, leaf, and small artificial fruit, to small pick; dip end of pick in glue and insert into cone. Place close together until surface is covered, then top with bird. Spray complete tree with gold spray. To make this tree appropriate for a silver wedding, spray with silver. Bronze and copper floral sprays are also available.

PRESSING FOR PERMANENCE

Pressing flowers is another sure method of preserving them and although they lose their three-dimensional quality, they are useful in many ways.

Place the material to be dried between many thicknesses of newspaper or between pages of old telephone books or catalogues (Figure 8E). To hasten matters, change the newspapers often. I have had satisfactory results in shortening the time by putting the newspapers or phone books on top of the clothes dryer or my husband's hi-fi system which is always warm. Normal drying time is 3-4 weeks.

Plate 14 illustrates a pressed flower picture which makes a quaint and charming gift.

The flowers were pressed by a somewhat different technique. First they were put between blotters and weights, then the top blotter removed and flowers allowed to dry in open air for 3 or 4 hours daily. The arranger feels that color and texture preservation were thereby improved. The pressed flowers were glued on 8x10″ background paper. The mat and frame increase the overall size to 11x14″.

Foliage can also be pressed this way, although with leaves you must place heavy books over the papers. Dried ferns need pressing under weights to prevent curling.

Plate 14 Pressed flower pictures make particularly lovely gifts. The flowers used for this rectangular picture are four two-toned fuchsias, two small yellow and orange marigolds, yellow perennial asters and small dark sprays of heather "Mrs. Beale."
Arranged by Mrs. Albert Downing (Photo same)

GLYCERINIZING LEAVES

Another way to preserve foliage is with glycerin and water. Glycerinized leaves are wonderful in arrangements (Plate 15) and, as a gift, are much appreciated by flower arrangers. A well shaped branch or two cut from barberry, magnolia, rhododendron, laurel, beech, crab apple tree, etc. is a lovely decoration, even while it is taking the glycerin bath (Figure 8F).

The procedure is simple: Mash the end of the twig with a hammer and slash the end four or five times, about two inches high at the base. Mix one part glycerin to two parts water, and pour six inches of mixture into a container. (I use a simple chemists flask but a milk bottle or quart mayonnaise jar would do, as would any vase).

Let the foliage stand in this mixture from two to five weeks. You should have no trouble deciding when the glycerin has been absorbed since most leaves take on a mahogany color and look shiny. The glycerin can be used time and again, and the glycerinized material lasts for many years. Allow 2 to 5 weeks for the whole process.

Plate 15   A striking arrangement of long-lasting dried material destined to give its recipient many hours of pleasure. The wooden container with its slightly burned grained base is especially appropriate in color and texture with the glycerinized magnolia leaves, and dried mullein, millet, and palm embryo.   *Arranged by Mrs. Robert E. Creighton*

SKELETONIZING LEAVES

Skeletonized leaves (Plate 16) called Angel Feathers by florists, can be prepared at home. The procedure is little more complicated than the ones discussed earlier in this chapter.

1. Prepare a solution of 1 teaspoon of baking soda to each quart of water. Boil leaves in this for about half an hour; allow them to remain in solution until it cools.

2. Remove leaves and spread them on a newspaper, then gently brush away the fleshy part of the leaf with a toothbrush or a dull knife.

3. Prepare a solution of 2 tablespoons of bleach to one quart of water; soak the leaves in it for an hour and a half, then rinse with clear water. Dry gently by patting with facial tissues. Press between the pages of a telephone book for a day or two.

Another way to skeletonize leaves involves less work, more time. Wrap glycerin-treated leaves in wax paper for a few months, then remove the leafy portion with a soft brush. Skeletonized leaves appear fragile but are sturdy and long lasting.

Pltae 16   Delicate skeletonized magnolia leaves are featured in a lovely dried arrangement. The Angel Feathers are grouped at the base of the design; the others are glued to painted willow branches for line, and the satiny-white lunaria seed pods point up the center of interest: the Goddess of Mercy.
Arranged by Mrs. Howard Oberlin   *(Photo Howard Oberlin)*

Plate 17   This contemporary Christmas panel could become a traditional part of a friend's holiday decorations. The frame is a dull gold and the background for the design is rich brown velvet which has been applied to a piece of thin plywood. The crescent line was formed from dried grey-brown eucalyptus foliage with natural beige oak leaves providing the transition material to the baby wood roses and dried edible artichokes. Sprayed very lightly with gold paint, gold glitter puffs and brown and gold ribbon are added to glamour-ize it.
Arranged by Mrs. Joe E. Wolff   *(Photo Joe E. Wolff)*

DRYING FRUITS AND VEGETABLES

Fruits and vegetables are easy to dry. Lemons, oranges, limes, tangerines, pomegranates, peppers, globe artichokes, and mushrooms are among the most popular of the dried fruits and vegetables. Give them during the harvest season, to be used as part of a doorway decoration, on gift packages, or in table centerpieces.

Wash and dry the material, store in a cool dry place on a rack such as used for roasting or cake-cooling.

The edible dried artichokes in Plate 17 were first dried, then lightly sprayed with gold, since the panel was intended for Christmas giving. As with all material to be dried or preserved, start with perfect specimens; preservation does not conceal blemishes.

WAXED FLOWERS AND FRUIT

While not as long-lasting as dried ones, waxed flowers and fruits have a special appeal and may be used in many charming ways. Wax arrangements will last much longer if kept under glass in an apothecary jar, under an old Victorian bell, or in a hurricane chimney (Plate 18).

Dissolve two blocks of colorless paraffin (available at hardware stores) and when fluid but not too hot, dip in freshly cut flowers or fruit holding them by the stem. Gently rotate them for a few moments until they are completely covered. Be sure to use a double boiler or a coffee can set in a skillet of water to minimize the fire and splatter hazard. Hang on line with clothespins until dry. Paper underneath will catch drippings.

Leftover candles may be used instead of, or combined with, the paraffin. For fruit with a translucent quality, add one white crayon when the wax is nearly melted.

Plate 18 An old-fashioned and charming gift reminiscent of Grandmother's days: fresh camellias, iris and hyacinths from the garden are waxed for long-lasting beauty and displayed to perfection in a hurricane chimney.
Arranged by Mrs. H. Jefferson Davis   *(Photo B. E. Johnson)*

SEED MOSAICS

Seeds in themselves have long held a special place in ancient folklore. Useful for propagation, of course, they are contemporary favorites in the making of seed mosaics (Plate 19). The procedure is quite simple. Leftover seeds from garden packets, and material from the garden or kitchen shelves —beans, rice, lentils, barley, split peas, poppy seeds, caraway and dill, are heated separately in muffin tins or aluminum plates, in a 350° F. oven. This prevents sprouting and attacks from insects. After fifteen minutes they are ready to use.

Have a piece of plywood or sturdy cardboard cut to the desired dimension. Rough in your design. A felt marking pen is ideal for plywood because it makes rather bold outlines. Apply white glue with a brush over small areas and fill in with seeds according to the design; tweezers will help you in some of the sections where you are working in fine detail. When the mosaic is completed and thoroughly dry, spray it with white shellac or several coats of clear plastic. A wooden frame completes the artistic gift.

One friend with patience and skill specializes in tiny seed mosaics made on lightweight cork backgrounds. Taken to a jeweler or hobby shop, they are inexpensively mounted as earrings and pendants . . . truly fascinating and personal gifts.

Plate 19 A seed mosaic fitted to the décor of a new house would make a most welcome housewarming gift. *Abstract design executed by Karl Mann Associates.*

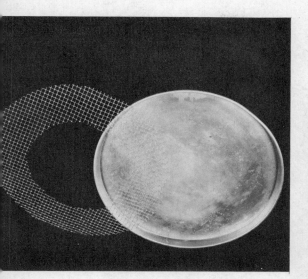

Plates 20 and 21   For a holiday gift, cones, seed pods, dried flowers, and nuts are secured to a circle of hardware cloth which is then fastened to a pizza pan with floral clay. Thoroughly spray the finished piece with flat-white, gold, copper spray or any color desired.
Arranged by Mrs. John S. Kestel

CONES AND PODS

Pine cones and seed pods may be painted, gilded, shellacked or used naturally in making many decorative articles. The table centerpiece made for a Christmas hostess began with a 12-inch pizza pan and a circle of hardware cloth 12-inches in diameter (Plates 20 and 21). Cones, seed pods, dried flowers and nuts were sprayed after they had been wired. For a Thanksgiving gift, a few colored leaves could be substituted for the evergreens at the rim, and a gilded dried pineapple could replace the candle.

Plate 22 A Please Open *Before* Christmas Gift could be a holiday plaque. Dried teasle cones, seed pods, gilded nuts and leaves, florist's wire, and hardware cloth with ribbon used for hanging, are the ingredients. *(Photo Jeannette Grossman)*

Non-perishable wreaths, swags, tiny trees can be enjoyed year after year. The materials for making a hanging plaque are shown in Plate 22. Small cones and seed pods make everlasting corsages (Plate 3) and are clever toppings for a gift package (Plate 52). Cones may be cut crosswise to resemble flowers or fashioned into owl decorations (Plate 23). The owls would be an amusing graduation tribute to honor newly acquired "wisdom." Seed pods are also tremendously versatile. Dried pods of the tulip tree were formed into poinsettias (Plate 24). Elsewhere through the book seed pods are shown in many different uses.

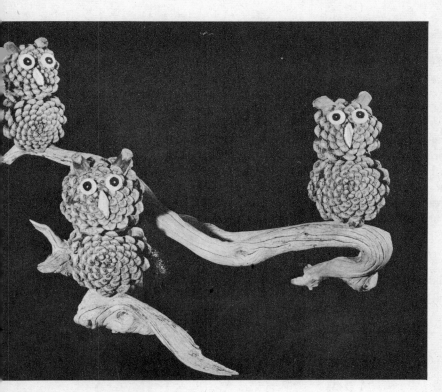

Plate 23 Two cones are glued together, the flat bottom of the cone towards the front. This makes the body and head. Two cone scales are inserted and glued for ears. Eyes can be any type of buttons. This arranger used plain white pearl buttons with a small black circle glued on in the center. The beak is a tiny triangle of yellow construction paper. The owls are secured to driftwood with posey clay.
Arranged by Mrs. Howard Oberlin
(Photo Howard Oberlin)

Plate 24 Dried pods of the tulip tree are made into poinsettia flowers. The lines are dried kelp, the leaves are from the Magnolia trees, and the centers are of deer moss and pearly everlasting weed. Framed in charcoal with a white and charcoal background, this hanging arrangement makes a striking and impressive gift.
Arranged by Mrs. Joe E. Wolff   (Photo Joe E. Wolff)

GOURDS FOR GIFTS, Fig. 9

Just as they are, gourds are splendid autumn gifts. They are handsome in baskets (Plate 25) or in wood, pottery, or old pewter containers. Fun to make and a welcome decoration are patio or charm strings (Figure 9). These probably originated with the Navajo Indians who hung similar strings outside their huts to bring good luck. In making them, use as many different articles and colors as possible. String a heavy gourd at one end of a heavy cord and then fill in with such natural materials as other colorful gourds, pine cones, bright peppers, dried fruits, seed pods, nuts, fragrant bunches of herbs, and pomander balls. Bird houses and dippers are useful little home made gifts from gourds.

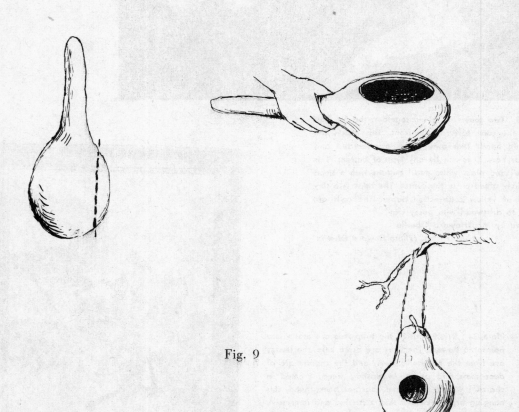

Fig. 9

Plate 25   Colorful gourds in an attractive garden basket would be a welcome autumn gift.
(*Photo Jeannette Grossman*)

Preserving Gourds

Gourds are annuals and may be grown on arbors, pergolas, and trellises. Obtain seed from the gourds themselves, dry them and plant the following year. Seeds are also available in packets, of course.

Ornamental gourds retain their brilliant coloring when dried, but may survive no more than 4 or 5 months. Hard-shelled lagenaria are known to have lasted as long as a hundred years; they offer many possibilities for decoration and for craft use.

After harvesting the ripe gourds, wash and scrub both types in a strong solution of non-bleaching household disinfectant such as borax. Put the ornamentals out of the sun to dry for ten days to two weeks. When thoroughly dry, apply a liquid floor wax to preserve their natural color.

The lagenarias take much longer to dry, sometimes several months, depending on their size and shape. Hang them or dry on racks in a cool dry place. If you do not want a mosaic-type design on the surface, watch them carefully for mold which must be washed off with a strong solution of borax.

Shaping and Decorating Hard-Shelled Gourds

The lagenarias may actually be shaped and decorated as they grow. Carve them when they are still on the vine, and shape them by tying raffia or soft tape around them. They may be grown inside flasks or plaster of paris molds.

Once the gourds are thoroughly dry, color them in any of a variety of ways. You may paint them with artist's tube color using varnish instead of oil, or, for a brush-painted design, use water color. They may be dyed with a fast dye, using a stronger solution than for fabrics. Dry them after the dye bath, then polish with paste wax.

Part of the fun of gourds is that an infinite number of techniques can be used to ornament them. Decorate with an electric pen, or burn on a design with a candle. With a nail or similar object, you can indent the design. The resist-brush technique of putting on the design before painting the surface is also worth trying. Whatever method you use, you will agree that making gifts from gourds can be fun for the whole family.

DRIFTWOOD FOR GIVING

Driftwood is actually a term for weathered wood found on mountains, in forests, along lakes and streams, near oceans, and even in one's own backyard. Many books have been written about this fascinating hobby, but the technique is actually quite simple. Finished wood can be made into lamps, tables, wall brackets, garden sculpture, planters and containers, as well as parts of the arrangement. Plates 26, 39 and 49 show some of the uses for weathered wood.

Finishing Wood for Decorative Purposes

1. Trim off any twiggy branches which are superfluous to the design as you visualize it. If there are rotted areas, chisel them out.

2. Clean the wood with mild soap suds, rinse with clear water and dry with a cloth. Let stand until completely dry.

3. Apply a coat of thin clear shellac which will pick up but not conceal the natural color of the wood. Furniture wax, shoe polish and even chalk may replace the shellac for different effects.

4. Pickling gives a spectacular finish. Brush white paint into the wood grain, then wipe it lightly. Apply thinned clear shellac when the paint is dry.

When you have preserved the natural beauty of the wood, you can present it as is, or make it into any of the decorative objects mentioned earlier.

Plate 26 Gnarled driftwood serves as a container for yellow gourds and dried okra pods. Pliable broom twigs are easy to shape into desired curves.　*(Photo Jeannette Grossman)*

PHOTOGRAMS

Amateur photographers who develop their own pictures can apply their hobby to making photograms (Plate 27) which are an attractive basis for greeting cards, book plates, place cards and framed pictures.

1. Collect ferns, leaves, flowers, and other natural materials and arrange them attractively.

2. In the darkroom, place your arrangement of materials on a sheet of photographic printing paper. There are many types you can use, depending on the effect you like, but double weight paper is recommended for the photograms.

3. Expose the paper to light, then develop the print in the normal procedure for any photograph.

Plate 27   Even weeds are a charming source of design for photograms. Use them as the basis for a greeting card, book plate, or room divider screen.   *(Photogram Robert Schneider)*

Plate 28 A plaque which shows the many possibilities for laminating garden materials in plastic, this collection of leaves was designed and executed by Harrington and Brown of Carmel, California.
(Photo Steve James)

EMBEDDING PLANT MATERIAL IN PLASTIC

Plant material embedded in plastic has a gift potential which is limited only by the imagination of the craftsman. Herbs, grasses, seed pods, berries, weeds, ferns, twigs, circles of wood and bamboo, even butterflies and tiny stones, can be embedded in plastic, in many useful and decorative articles.

The Flower Show held recently by the Lake Forest (Illinois) garden club, featured popular and salable gifts prepared by a committee of club members. Coasters, trays, miniature key rings, place mats, and protectors for light switches and door panels were made from thin plastic sheets between which were embedded dried herbs and flowers.

The plaque shown in Plate 28 features only leaves, but the basic procedure applies to all plant materials. This technique is easier and less complicated than it seems, see Fig. 10.

Tools: scissors, measuring spoons, knife, tweezers, eyedropper, pencil, paper cups, ruler, a piece of cardboard.

Materials: 2 pieces heavyweight laminating mat; 2 pieces laminating film—2 inches longer and 2 inches wider than the pieces of mat; liquid laminating plastic, such as Castoglas, hardener, pressed flowers, foliage, weeds, ferns.

A. Arrange plant material on a paper pattern in an attractive design. Place one sheet of laminating film on a smooth surface such as a piece of glass or a level table, and place one section of mat on the film, so that the film is one inch larger than the mat on all sides.

B. Fill a paper cup with amount of liquid plastic and hardener needed,

C. Transfer design to the wet mat; cover with another mat. Soak the second mat with more of the mixture of plastic and hardener.

Cover with the remaining sheet of laminating film, and smooth with a piece of cardboard to make sure the plastic resin is evenly distributed, and to insure a smooth surface without bubbles. The four layers are shown in the drawing.

D. The plaque will begin to harden within 30 minutes. After an hour trim the edges evenly with a sharp knife, using the rule to guide you. Remove the laminating film, and sand edges with a fine sandpaper.

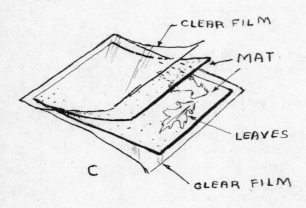

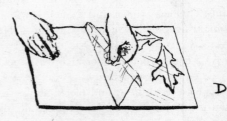

Fig. 10

4

gifts from your home nursery

Many plants are easily propagated from seeds and cuttings, or by division and layering, giving you an inexpensive source of presents as well as a creative hobby. Also, plants you grow yourself can be rare kinds which are not commercially cultivated for one reason or another. Rarity is a much-appreciated quality in gift plants.

PROPAGATING BY SEED

With seeds you can propagate annual herbs, bromeliads, succulents, gourds, wildflowers, miniature roses, alpines, new and unusual varieties of vegetables, camellias, and other shrubs. There are several advantages of sowing seeds yourself, although time is not one of them. There is economy, first, and then the special thrill of starting a plant from seed and watching its complete development. The technique for growing plants from seed is relatively simple.

Fill the container with slightly moistened soil. Settle soil by tapping the container on a bench. Press soil down about ½ inch from the rim with the bottom of a drinking glass or with a brick if the container is large.

Press seed gently into the soil about ¼-inch deep or twice the diameter of the seed. Water thoroughly.

When the second or third set of leaves appear, the plants are ready for their first move. Dampen soil before removing the seedlings. Prepare the new soil by tamping it, leveling it, and then slightly dampening it.

Remove the seedlings gently with a fork and plant them two to three inches apart, placed a trifle lower in the soil than they were before. (Or follow instructions on seed packet.) Firm soil gently after planting. Spray to water.

When the plants are three to five inches tall, they are ready to pot and give or to move into the garden. After transplanting, the plants need partial shade, then sun.

If you start your seeds in peat pots, the shock of transplanting will be considerably lessened as the roots are not disturbed when pot and all are planted. Peat pots may be bought in colorful plastic containers which make your gift attractive and easily-wrapped.

THE EASIEST CUTTINGS ARE STEM CUTTINGS

Many house plants will root easily. The simplest way is to cut off the fresh new tips of the plants, remove the lower leaves and flowers, and put the tips into water, or into a mixture of sand and peat moss. (In summer the cuttings may be set right into the garden.) Give the cuttings light but not sun, keep them watered (Fig. 14), and they will be off to a good start. When roots have developed, plant cuttings in a 3″ pot in a general soil mixture. The plants will be ready for giving in less than 2 months from the time you first took the cutting.

Plants that will root easily from cuttings are ivy, grape ivy, kangaroo vine, begonia, philodendron, episcia, coleus, tradescantia, and geraniums (Plate 29). To propagate strawberry begonia and spider plant, set the little plants which grow at the ends of runners into 3″ flower pots.

Most of the plants shown in Plate 30 are easily propagated by cutting. A whole windowful of them would make a valuable housewarming gift. Single potted plants are a thoughtful "get well" present; cacti and succulents require little care and are very useful for giving to busy people.

Plate 29   Geranium cuttings taken in late summer and placed in rooting medium make good gifts for gardeners. This is one of the fancy-leaved varieties.   (Photo Jeannette Grossman)

Plate 30 Most of the plants in this window are easily propagated by cutting. Bird cage is filled with philodendron; the natural coconut shells are planted with spider plant. Monkey tail is the top right plant in wall bracket, strawberry begonias are lower right. Left wall brackets hold wax plant (top) and grape ivy (below). Cacti on glass shelves in lower window. On window seat are African violets propagated by leaf cuttings, division and seed. Begonias, and paper-white narcissus are planted in pebbles.   *Home of Mrs. H. J. Mitchell*

MALLET AND LEAF CUTTINGS, Fig. 11

You may propagate some philodendrons and rubber plants by means of mallet cuttings. The mallet cutting is so called because it includes a stem and one leaf; it is handled the same as the stem cutting.

Leaf cuttings are a popular method of propagating African violets and certain succulents such as sedum and echeveria (Plates 31, 32). Insert leaves into a 1-1-1 mixture (see page 63) and proceed as for stem cuttings.

A variation of this method is to cut the leaf with an inch stalk, and with a sharp knife make cuts just below the point where the veins branch. Insert the stalk in the sand, and anchor the leaf flat with stones, toothpicks, or hairpins. New plants will form at the points where you severed the main veins.

A leaf may also be cut in pie-shaped pieces; each piece containing a main vein. These will root and produce plantlets.

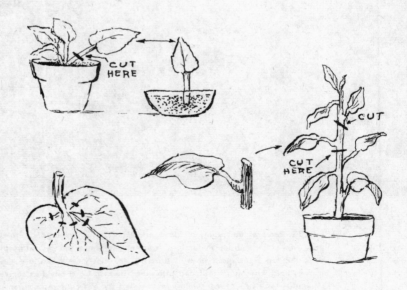

Fig. 11

e 31 Echeveria leaves, when potted in sand or
niculite, will form roots and new plants in a mat-
of a few weeks. Smaller leaves from the flowering
are used here. (Photo Arthur E. Luedy)

Plate 32 Succulents in pots make nice gifts for the
shut-in or apartment house dweller. Plants are easily
started in sandy soil. (Photo Jeannette Grossman)

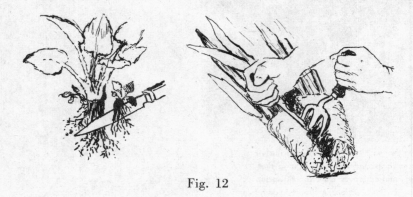

Fig. 12

PLANTS BY DIVISION, Fig. 12

Another good means of multiplying gift plants is to divide them. Division is probably the surest and easiest technique of propogation. When the plants are dormant, remove the soil ball from the container (or dig up from garden), gently shake off soil and pull or cut clumps apart. Repot in individual containers. African violets, hardy asters, chrysanthemums, ferns, bearded irises, oriental poppies, snake plants and succulents are easily divided.

Among the herbs, balm, chives, peppermint, spearmint, rue and tarragon divide well.

AIR LAYERING, Fig. 13

Air layering is recommended for many indoor and outdoor plants. Such comparatively costly ones as rhododendrons, and indoors hollies, dogwoods, dracaenas, dieffenbachias, and rubber plants, are all propagated by air layering. The procedure is far less technical than you suspect.

Notch either the stem or a branch (A). Dust the notched area with one of the hormone rooting powders, and wrap it in damp sphagnum moss (B). Wrap a sheet of plastic, wax paper, or aluminum foil tightly around the moss, and bind or tape both ends of the sack (C). Keep the moss moist.

For outdoor plants started in the spring, rooting will usually take place the following fall. The average rooting time for indoor plants is about eight weeks.

When rooting has taken place, cut off the layer directly below the sphagnum ball. Do not disturb the moss when potting and, when potted, keep in a shaded, cool place.

THE BASIC NEEDS, Fig. 14

Soil

If seeds or cuttings are planted in containers, you will be better able to control the soil conditions than if planted in open ground outdoors. A good general potting mix is known as the 1-1-1 mix: ⅓ garden soil or compost, ⅓ sharp sand, ⅓ peat moss and/or leaf mold. These should be mixed thoroughly and should be slightly damp when used. Bring a quantity of garden soil or compost indoors before the rains come so that you will have a supply for potting.

Container

Even if new, containers should be scrubbed clean and immersed in boiling water for at least five minutes. Be sure that the container has holes for drainage; cover these with pieces of broken crockery or squares of window screening (A and B). Next comes a layer of gravel, broken crockery, or sand, and then the potting mix.

Procedure

1. Hormones stimulate the formation of roots on cuttings and vitamin B[1] promotes their growth once they start. Dust seeds with the hormone rooting powder before planting; dip the cuttings into water first, then into the powder, shaking off the excess.

Fig. 13

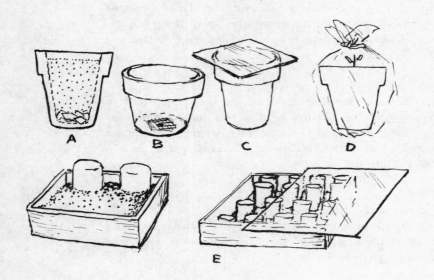

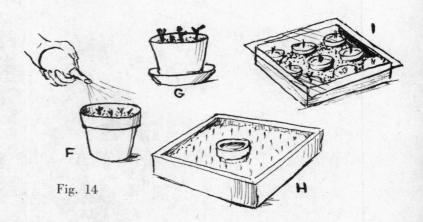

Fig. 14

2. Water at time of planting with a complete plant food, and two or three times a week, thereafter.

3. Cover the seed containers with canvas, burlap, a sheet of glass or plastic and newspapers to provide warmth and darkness (C).

Or, put individual pots of cuttings into plastic bags, closing the top with a rubber band (D).

Or, put a number of small cans or pots with seeds in a box whose sides are slightly higher than the containers; cover with a square of glass and then with newspapers to keep the light out until the sprouts begin to show (E).

4. Provide heating for the bottom of the container. I have used the top of my automatic clothes dryer to produce this heat with some success, and I know some who use the top of water heaters for the same purpose. Bottom heat may also be built in by outfitting a false bottom with an electric light bulb or with an electric cable.

5. Water thoroughly immediately after seed or cutting is planted and whenever top of soil is dry. A mulch of redwood sawdust or sifted sphagnum moss will help retain the moisture.

Water the top with a fine spray (F).Water from the bottom, standing the container in water (G).

If you are using a flat or a large clay pot for the container, place a clay pot in the middle of it, first sealing its drainage hole with a piece of gum or clay. When soil needs water, pour water into the pot. This method prevents washing away seed and allows gradual distribution of the water (H).

If you are using a number of small pots, plunge them into a box containing peat moss which is kept damp (I). This arrangement may be covered with plastic or glass. The same principle will work with a small clay pot inserted into a larger one.

FORCED BULBS

In the dead of winter, give a pot of flowering bulbs in an attractive jardiniere to herald the coming of spring, (Plates 33 and 34). This is one gift which you really must plan ahead. Buy the best bulbs you can find in October. Roman hyacinths, however, may be purchased as soon as late August or early September for bloom in November. Look for varieties particularly recommended for forcing. Tulips, hyacinths and daffodils are most popular but crocus, planted thickly in a shallow pot, makes a gay window sill decoration. For a friend who likes the scent and hue of violets, force a few bulbs of iris reticulata. Checkered lily (*Fritillaria meleagris*) grape hyacinths, glory of the snow, Siberian squill, snowdrops, spring snowflake, and winter aconite are all recommended for forcing.

Plate 33 Pot of forced dwarf daffodils, *Narcissus obvallaris*, with deep yellow trumpet flowers on eight-inch stems. It is often called the Tenby daffodil. Outdoors it is early-flowering, sturdy, and lasting, fine for colonizing. (*Photo Bernice Brilmayer*)

Plate 34 Potting dwarf daffodils to be forced, with light, porous soil lightly enriched with bone meal. A gift of flowering bulbs, for winter-time giving must be planned in the fall. Don't forget to label and date them. (*Photo Bernice Brilmayer*)

POTTING PROCEDURE

1. A six-inch bulb pan is usually used for this procedure. Clean thoroughly and soak.

2. Use a 1-1-1 mixture for potting, or pot in a good garden soil mixed with a dusting of bonemeal and some leafmold.

Provide for drainage by covering the drainage holes with squares of window screening or pieces of broken crockery, and a first layer of sand, broken crockery, or gravel.

3. Fill pot ⅔ full of soil, place the bulbs on it 1 inch apart. Cover with more soil mix and press down firmly. The noses of the bulbs should be just below the soil's surface.

4. Water thoroughly. Label, and date.

5. Store pots in a well-drained trench in your garden, or in a cellar if the temperature there is 40° or below. This storage is necessary in order for the bulbs to develop a healthy root structure.

6. In late November or early December examine the pots. If the roots show through the drainage hole, the pots are ready to bring indoors to light and a temperature of 50° F. Here they should stay for a few weeks until the bulbs develop flower stems. To flower, the bulbs will then need a temperature of 65°, good light, and some sunshine.

7. Bulbs may not be forced two years in a row, but they may be planted out in the garden in spring if, after flowering, dead blooms are removed and watering is continued until the leaves begin to turn yellow.

WATER CULTURE

Hyacinths are the bulbs to use for this; special containers were even devised for this procedure called hyacinth glasses.

Place bulbs in the containers, and fill them with water which reaches just to the base of the bulb.

Store in a dark, airy place at a temperature of 45 to 50° until the containers are well filled with roots.

Then bring into a light room which has a temperature of 65° for flowering.

After flowering, discard the bulbs.

PEBBLE CULTURE

Paper White and Soleil d'Or Narcisi and Chinese Sacred Lilies are bulbs that will grow in pebbles.

Use a container about 5 inches deep and 7 inches in diameter. Fill it half-full of small, ½-inch in diameter pebbles, and place bulbs on the pebbles. Fill to within 1 inch of the rim with more pebbles.

When you water, remember that it must reach to the base of the bulbs. Whenever necessary, replenish the water.

Plate 35 Christmas gifts for gardeners. Heathers in your garden produce rooted branches which may be cut from the parent plants. In November plant several of these rooted branches in a pot of peaty loam and sand. Keep in a cool frost-free place until Christmas. This is the popular early blooming heather called Springwood White.　　*(Photo Jeannette Grossman)*

Store containers in a cool, airy place for three or four weeks when you may bring them in for flowering.

These, too, must be discarded after forcing.

TENDER BULBS

Tender bulbs such as amaryllis and callas also make lovely gifts during the winter. As this is their natural time for blooming, this is not really forcing and there is no need for storage.

Pot these bulbs and keep in dim light until top growth starts, when they are brought into a light room for flowering.

During the summer plunge the pots out of doors in the garden. Then bring them inside to rest during the fall in a dark, dry place such as the cellar, and allow the foliage to dry off.

GIFT PLANTS AND BULBS FROM THE GARDEN

At summer's end, lift plants from your garden to give as gifts. Heather (Plate 35), chrysanthemums, geraniums and many herbs are pleasant possibilities.

Bulbs increase rapidly in the garden. When foliage is dead, lift them with a digging fork by digging straight down to a good depth. Shake off soil. Dry bulbs in the garage or in a protected spot in your garden. Clean, separate them, label and store. About February, start the bulbs if they are to be planted outdoors. Give bulbs already started in flats (Plate 36) or sometime in January put them into pots to be enjoyed in full bloom indoors in May.

Be sure to label your gift, and give instructions on planting bulbs or discarding them after they flower.

FORCING EARLY BLOOM

Many a bride who received duplicate electric percolators or silver bread trays would have preferred a gift of flowering branches to decorate the place where the wedding ceremony was held. Masses of forced forsythia, arranged in twin containers for each side of an altar, offer marvelous contrast against the dark wood of many country churches. Big bunches of quince would be appreciated at a small home wedding, their pastel prettiness so appropriate to the simplicity of the occasion.

Plate 36   Begonia tubers already started in a flat of soil will be welcomed by most garden-ers. Start dormant tubers in March and they can be transplanted outdoors in May. In most areas, tubers should be lifted again in November, labeled and stored to be started again the following year. Give instructions with your gift.   *(Photo Jeannette Grossman)*

The procedure for forcing branches to flower early is relatively easy. Prune the shrubs or trees on a mild day in winter or early spring, preferably after a rain. Hammer the ends of heavy branches, then soak the whole branch for 24 hours. Keep in a container of water in a dark room until the buds break open; they are then ready to be transferred to someone's sunny window for flowering. The branches may be made into flower arrangements before or after they are forced.

	If cut in	Will flower in
Andromeda	early February	3-4 weeks
	mid-March	1-2 weeks
Azalea	end of January or early February	3-6 weeks
Bridal Wreath	mid-March	4 weeks
Daphne	late January	2-3 weeks
Deutzia	mid-March	5-6 weeks
Flowering Almond Cherry, Plum	mid-March	2-3 weeks
Flowering Dogwood	mid-March	2-4 weeks
Forsythia	early January	3 weeks
	early February	2 weeks
Honeysuckle	early March	1-2 weeks
Japanese Maple	early March	2 weeks
	mid-March	1 week
Kerrybush	early March	2½ weeks
Leucothoe	March	4-5 weeks
Lilac	early March	4-5 weeks
Mock-Orange	mid-March	4-5 weeks
Mountain Laurel	mid-March	5 weeks
Pussy Willow	February	1-2 weeks
Quince, Japanese or Flowering	early February	3-4 weeks
Rhododendron	February or March	4-6 weeks
Wisteria	mid-March	5 weeks

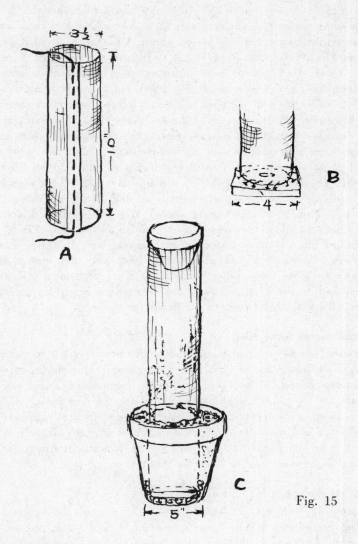

Fig. 15

Forced flowers are at their best for only a few days. If you are creating forced material as a gift for a specific occasion and date, it is best to stagger the cutting of branches, that is, cut a supply every few days so you can be certain to have blooms when needed.

Flowering time can be speeded up by putting the budded branches in a sunny light room. Flowering can be retarded by keeping the branches in a cool dark room.

MAKING A MOSS STICK

A moss stick is an impressive gift. Although costly when bought, it can be made quite easily. Use vining plants such as scindapsus, pothos, large-leaved variegated ivy or trailing philodendron. A container about 8 inches in diameter is a good size. Root 4 or 5 strands of vine, at least 4 inches each, in water. Roll quarter-inch hardware cloth—3 feet wide and 10 inches long—into a cylinder about 3½ inches in diameter. Fasten with wire (A). Nail bottom of cylinder to a heavy piece of wood of the right size to fit snugly into the bottom of the container (B). The wood should have a drainage hole drilled into the base. Line cylinder with peat moss which has been thoroughly soaked. A half-and-half mix of peat moss and vermiculite may be substituted. Add two inches of gravel, then fill container with regular planting soil. Put a small clay pot, its drainage hole plugged with clay, into the top of the cylinder and fill it with water (C). With a pencil make 4 holes evenly spaced around the stick. Plant the rooted vines (by now they may have doubled in length). Circle the vines around the cylinder, fastening at intervals with hairpins. Fasten new shoots to cylinder to maintain shape. Keep clay pot in top filled with water so moss stays moist. Turn plant frequently so all sides get even light but do not keep in strong sun. The gift is ready for presentation when the vines have covered the hardware cloth.

AN AFRICAN VIOLET TOTEM POLE

If African-violets fill most of your window sills and overflow to porches, make a few totem poles to give. Use the procedure for the moss stick but substitute 2-inch chicken wire for the hardware cloth, and 4 pounds sphagnum and ½ pound granulated charcoal for the peat moss. Moisten the moss with a water-soluble fertilizer solution before planting the "violets"—you will need about 20 of them. After washing off soil, wrap the roots in a ball of moist sphagnum before planting it firmly in the pole. Feed with water-soluble fertilizer through pot at top of pole.

TRAINING IVY ON FORMS

Propagating ivy cuttings in water or sand is one of the simplest of gardening procedures, which is fortunate, since ivy is also one of the most useful of plants for making gifts. Small varieties are fine in dish gardens and terraria. The vine can be trained to grow on driftwood, espaliered on a small trellis in a pot, used in making corsages and wreaths, and even glycerinized. Hardy varieties should be slected for pots which are to be used outdoors all year around, but many non-hardy varieties are useful for indoor training.

An ivy Christmas Tree (Fig. 16) is a unique gift. Tie 4 sticks in a tepee shape and fit into a container . . . a large clay pot would be fine.

Each stick should be about 2½ times the height of the container. Fill container with an inch or two of gravel, then with a porous mixture of peat, humus, sand and top soil. With a pencil make a little hole near each tepee stick and plant ivy on each one. Train into tree shape by tying new shoots to form with nylon thread or Twistems. Feed during the growing period with a fertilizer high in nitrogen and potash. Few ivies do well in direct sun and all require moisture. A gift of two matching ivy forms will be eye-catching, attractive and long lasting.

SUCCULENT GARDEN IN A STRAWBERRY JAR

Give a house plant requiring little upkeep to a friend whose time is at a premium, especially if she longs to grow things. Cacti and other succulents thrive on neglect and can tolerate our overheated houses. Their interesting forms, colors and blooms give continuing pleasure, Plate 37.

Provide drainage by placing a wire screen square over the drainage hole. Add two or three inches of drainage material such as pebbles or broken crocks. Use a mix for succulents—2 parts coarse sand, 1 part garden soil, 1 part leaf mold, and ½ part granulated charcoal, and keep mix on dry side when planting. Fill the top and pockets with succulents: Cobweb sempervivum, Echeveria Elegans, Sedum Guatemalense, Crassula nodulosa, and Sedum spathulifolium combine well. Withhold water for several days, then water only lightly for the first two months. After plants are established, check soil to a depth of ½ inch and when this is dry, water.

Fig. 16

5

bonsai, miniature landscapes, dish gardens and terraria

Few can resist the appeal of a small-scale dish garden or bonsai—a gnarled and stunted shrub, tree or vine grown in a container. There's nothing mysterious about growing them—the uncertainty involves whether you can bear to part with your miniature, even to give to someone you dearly love. Perhaps you had better make at least two!

Years ago, when people did not move around so much, there was a charming custom of planting a tree to commemorate a baby's birth . . . this custom can be revived with bonsai. Properly cared for, a bonsai will give pleasure not only to mother, but to baby when he is grown. To insure the plant's survival, give written cultural directions for its care.

Many of us are familiar with the little oriental ming trees sold by florists before the second World War. In essence, they are merely imitations of bonsai, although extremely popular in their time. Later, bonsai became widely known in our country, but the American version is not according to tradition. We do not have the infinite skill and patience of the Japanese, who may spend anywhere from 10 to 200 years on their specimens, handing them down as a precious legacy from one generation to the next.

Japanese classify trees according to size, style and shape. If the shape of the tree is erect and natural looking, it is designated as a *chokkan* bonsai (Fig. 17 bottom). If trunk is slanting, it is called *shakon* (Fig. 17 top) if gnarled, *hankon*. One of the most attractive styles is the cascade or drooping style called *kengai*.

Although lacking authenticity and tradition, the American bonsai satisfies our needs because it can be done relatively quickly. With a few procedures for pruning roots and branches, and some wiring technique you can grow marvelous bonsai to give as extraordinary presents.

74

Fig. 17

THE FIRST POTTING

I save shallow tin cans for bonsai—coffee cans hold a plant about six inches tall; a fruit cake tin about eight inches tall. If you are making a "slow" bonsai, somewhat in traditional style, I advise you not to start with a plant much bigger than eight inches. Punch three holes for drainage in the bottom of the can, using a juice opener. Cover the holes with some screening, sprinkle a quarter-inch layer of gravel over the screen, then add about half an inch of soil mixture. Trim off some of the roots, and pot immediately, gently spreading out the roots as you do so. Now sift soil lightly around the roots and tamp down with your fingers to be sure there are no air spaces. Sprinkle with water a few times a day for a few days. Let plants stay here for about six months before you transplant into a more permanent container and start more drastic pruning.

For A Quick Bonsai

Buy a plant up to 24 inches high in a tin container, Fig. 18A. Cut off the tin, wearing gloves for protection. Loosen dirt with a pointed stick (B), removing at least half. Trim off 1/3 of the roots (C). Pot into the container in which you will give the bonsai; be sure it has drainage holes, window screen, gravel and plant mix. Plant, add soil, tamp it down to make it firm and remove air pockets. Give with directions for its care.

THE SOIL

The soil requirements for bonsai depend, of course, on the type of plant you will be using. Make it a habit to ask the nurseryman what mix he recommends for each plant, and record it in your notebook.

Generally, evergreens will do well in a mixture of one-half subsoil to one-half parts sharp sand. Some people like to add a small amount of crushed limestone to this mix.

For other than evergreens a mixture of 1/3 garden loam, 1/3 clean sand, and 1/3 leaf mold or peat moss is a good general mix. Soil should be well sifted and thoroughly mixed.

SELECTING THE PERMANENT CONTAINER

The Japanese consider the container an integral part of the picture; it must harmonize in color, texture and scale with the plant it contains. It must have drainage holes and screening, gravel and soil as recommended under *The First Potting* (above).

GETTING PLANTS

The easiest way is to buy a plant from a nurseryman. Look for stunted asymmetrical growth, unusual shape and a heavy trunk. Already conditioned to living in small spaces, it probably will not die when transplanted. Ask the dealer to recommend plants whose flowers, berries and

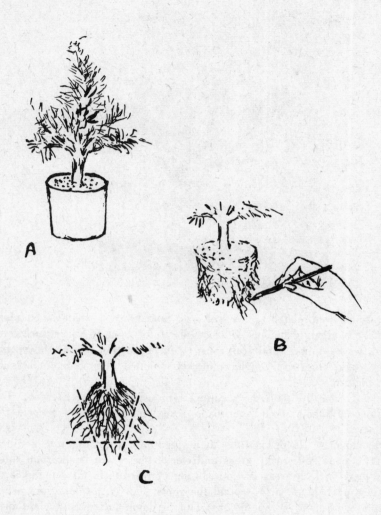

Fig. 18

Plate 37 Following the bonsai principle, this little succulent has been confined in the same
pot for over four years, and has been pruned into tree shape.   (Photo Steve James)

fruit are all well-related to the leaf size. Sometimes a small-leaved plant
will have a gigantic bloom, which spoils it for bonsai. For a successful
bonsai, leaves, flowers and fruit must be in proportion to each other and
to the trunk, otherwise you have merely a potted plant and not a landscape picture.

If you order by mail, the seedlings will usually arrive bareroot. The
container and soil should be made ready in advance to receive the
seedlings.

The Japanese favor getting their seedlings from natural settings.
Plants in poor soil, rocky areas and sterile places are better than those
which grow in lush areas. If you can get permission to take it, dig it up
with a good ball of earth around the roots. Fall is the best time, when
plants are dormant. Wrap the root ball in damp burlap and plant in a
tin can for a year or so before you move it into its container.

Among the plants which are useful, try azalea, bamboo, beech, birch,
boxwood, camellia, cedar, cherry, crabapple, cotoneaster, cypress, elm,
fir, ginko, hawthorne, holly, ivy, juniper, maple, oak, pine, pomegranate,
pyracantha, quince, redwood, spruce and willow. However, this is just a
partial list, and in American bonsai anything goes if it is suited in proportion. For a birthday or Christmas bonsai, I like to give an evergreen
tree for it symbolizes eternal life. Most of the conifers are well adapted
to bonsai; they are sturdy and survive well.

ROOT PRUNING

Follow the procedure shown in Fig. 18, *For A Quick Bonsai:* After removing the plant carefully from its temporary container, remove $\frac{1}{2}$ to $\frac{2}{3}$ of the old soil gently with a pointed stick. This operation should be done inside or in the shade. Trim off $\frac{1}{3}$ of the root length with a sharp scissors; the tap root or main root should have only $\frac{1}{4}$ of its length removed. While you are preparing the container, soak the exposed roots in water.

The drainage holes should be covered with a square of window screen or a piece of broken crockery, a layer of gravel, and then the mixed soil.

POTTING BONSAI

Carefully spread out the roots of the plant, and place the crown a little above the soil line. Fill in with the soil. With the end of a pencil or with chopsticks, gently push down into the soil to make sure that the soil comes into contact with the roots. Tamp down with your hands, firmly but gently, and then sprinkle until water runs from the drainage holes.

The plant should be kept inside or in a sheltered place for about two weeks, safe from wind and sun.

PRUNING

Pruning is both an art and a skill, and some will probably find it the most difficult aspect of bonsai. With wiring, it is used to emphasize the natural contours of the tree and to create an aged appearance. Since most trees do not grow in ideal conditions, the tree usually acquires an asymmetrical shape.

The Japanese have a very definite feeling about symmetry, and in most of their art since Zenism they have avoided symmetry because it expresses completion and repetition. Zen emphasizes the *process* of attaining perfection, rather than perfection itself, so perhaps we can emulate the Japanese, and, if we make mistakes in our pruning, let us believe that learning is just as important as attaining perfection. For after all, pruning is a lifetime study.

Now for the specifics. Your pruning shears should always be sharp, and I think your first concern in pruning should be the removal of dead and diseased wood, crossing or rubbing branches, and weak, narrow crotches, Fig. 19. After doing this I like to live with the plant awhile before I do any drastic pruning, perhaps sketching it to see the different effects possible, then wiring.

The pruning cuts should be made at a slight angle (30 to 45°) $\frac{1}{8}$ of an inch above the bud pointing in the direction you want the tree to develop. If there are two buds on a level, the cut should be as close to $\frac{1}{8}$ of an inch above these as possible. Do not leave stubs on the trunk after removing branches. They are extremely unattractive.

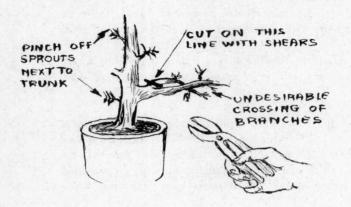

PINCH OFF SPROUTS NEXT TO TRUNK

CUT ON THIS LINE WITH SHEARS

UNDESIRABLE CROSSING OF BRANCHES

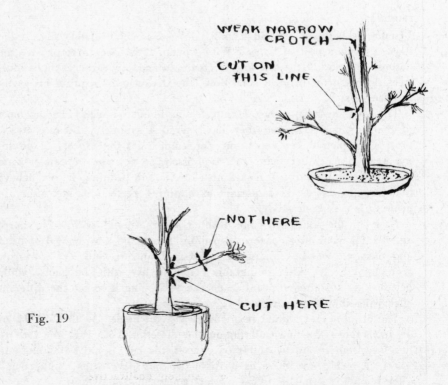

WEAK NARROW CROTCH

CUT ON THIS LINE

NOT HERE

CUT HERE

Fig. 19

WHEN TO PRUNE

The are two schools of thought about when to prune after planting. Some experts say it helps the tree to do it right away; others prefer waiting until the roots have time to get over the shock and adjust to their new environment.

I do a little necessary pruning when I first pot, and should more drastic pruning be required, usually wait for about two or three months before doing it.

I believe that if you prune properly, you should be able to do it practically all year round, although spring is considered by many as the ideal time.

Pruning deciduous trees, however, is best before the new spring growth appears. You can see more clearly what you are doing. And plants which flower *before* foliage appears, such as flowering cherries and almonds, should be pruned immediately after flowering.

Once your plants are established in the lines you want them, most pruning will be merely pinching off the new growth where you don't want it, leaving a couple of new green leaves behind. Experts also claim that pinching off leaves and cutting branches back to the dormant buds will result in smaller leaves.

WIRING YOUR BONSAI

Wiring your bonsai to shape it is the professional touch, best done in the springtime when the branches are supple. Wiring helps train the contours of the little trees, shortening and bending them in the direction you want them to go. For this I use insulated copper wire. The diameter of the wire depends on the strength of the trunk and the branches. I use No. 18 wire for light branches and No. 10 for heavy trunk wiring.

There are two methods of wiring, both of which you will use at one time or another: one is the spiral method and the other is what I call the hooking or latching method.

Spiral method: To shape trunk, insert one end of the wire in the soil at the same angle as the trunk and then wind it in even spirals one-half to one inch apart, Fig. 20. Using both hands, gently bend the trunk in the curve you desire, taking care not to jar the trunk and disturb the roots. To shorten and curve branches use the same technique. Fasten one end of the wire to the trunk. Instead of wire for very small and very young bonsai, I have often used plant ties. Trunk and fork wiring by the spiral method are shown in the drawing.

Latching method: Hook one end of the wire to the trunk and the other end to the branch bringing them closer together at different points. For an interesting variation of this method, arc the tree over the side of the container cascade-fashion. Latch one end of the wire to the tree and the other to the drainage hole.

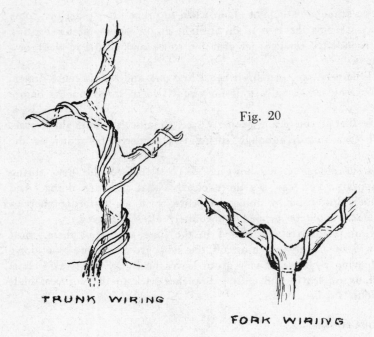

Fig. 20

TRUNK WIRING

FORK WIRING

The wire is left on for six months to a year and then gently unwound or detached. If, at this time, the curve is not stationary or the way you want it, wind it up again for another few months. Patience and persistence are the keys to successful bonsai.

ACCESSORIES FOR BONSAI

Stones, pebbles, moss, baby tears, and occasionally driftwood are the only accessories used in the true bonsai. Your imagination is supposed to fill in the rest.

Moss helps give a very aged appearance quickly, and the soft velvety green is very pleasing to the eye and to the touch.

If you use a container without drainage holes, pebbles may be your answer. Use a shallow container and fill only two-thirds of it with soil, leaving one end free. Pebbles are put at this end and not only look scenic, but they also draw the excess water so that the tiny trees don't get wet feet, and enable you to see if you are over-watering (Fig. 21).

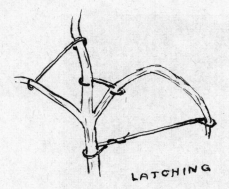

LATCHING

WATERING

Watering should be done with as fine a spray as possible. Use a child's sprinkling can, the bulb-type sprinkler, or an attachment on your hose.

Water at least once a day, more often if the weather is extremely hot, until the water runs out of the drainage holes. It should be done preferably in the morning, and the leaves should also be sprinkled.

FEEDING

This should be done moderately, only two or three times a year. Diluted liquid fish or manure tea are probably the best to use, though one bonsai expert uses a mixture of bone meal, dried blood, and cottonseed meal, rolling the mixture into little balls which he places on the soil near the rim of the container. Thus the plant would be fed very gradually whenever it is watered. Thoroughly moisten the soil before feeding and again afterwards.

TRANSPLANTING

Transplanting is really another method of feeding your bonsai by replenishing old worn-out soil with fresh nutrient-filled new soil. Evergreens should be transplanted every three or four years. Broadleaved evergreens, such as azaleas and camellias, should be transplanted every two years, and fruit trees every year.

The procedure is the same as for the original potting: do it in the shade; remove part of the old soil; trim the roots; and soak them while preparing the container.

At transplanting time the position of the tree can then be changed if you so desire. You might try, for instance, planting it at an angle.

Plate 38   A miniature landscape features two tiny bamboo plants in frozen-orange juice cans inserted into the soil of the planter.   *(Photo Steve James)*

COVER ALL BUT
ONE CORNER
OF THE TRAY
WITH A LAYER
OF PEBBLES

COVER PEBBLES
WITH SOIL

Fig. 21

DISH GARDENS AND LANDSCAPES

Miniature gardens and landscapes can be created with plant material that is naturally dwarf and slow growing. A variety of trees, shrubs, bulbs, ferns, annuals, perennials, succulents and even aquatic plants are available in dwarf form. You can create a landscape or scene from nature to suit almost every taste: a cactus garden, a formal rose garden (miniature roses including climbers are offered in the rose catalogs) or an evergreen garden. Fast growing seedlings with mature shapes can also be used, but they will have to be replaced when they have outgrown the landscape.

Dwarf conifers—cedar, false cypress, juniper, spruce, etc.—are the gems of any miniature collection and one of them could be the backbone of any landscape scene. They come in different shapes and different shades of green, and although not always easy to find, they are available and may be ordered by mail. Descriptive terms such as pygmaea, nana, and minima will tip you off to their small size.

The little conifers are fairly simple to propagate by taking cuttings in spring and autumn and inserting them in sharp sand. Friends who have never seen their likes before will be thrilled with a gift of a dwarf tree. These differ from bonsai in that they are naturally slow growers even in open ground, and do not need to be confined in pots or have their roots pruned. Their principal use has been in rock gardens and miniature gardens, although they have been used in American bonsai.

PLACE TREE ROOTS
IN SOIL AND PRESS
THE SOIL FIRMLY
WITH YOUR FINGERS

THEN TAMP DIRT
DOWN DEEP WITH
A STICK.

THE OPEN CORNER OF THE POT
WILL SUPPLY AIR AND SHOW
WHEN WATER SHOULD BE ADDED

The bonsai principle can be used in creating miniatures. Select perfectly proportioned material, small leaved and small blossomed, and keep it small by pruning and confining the roots in small cans such as used for baby food, frozen juices, and tuna fish. Insert the cans into the soil of the container. With this method you can rotate the plants at will, changing them as they outgrow their usefulness, and using together in one landscape plants which have different cultural requirements.

Giving a miniature dish garden is fun, but designing and executing it can be really soul-satisfying. At first, try your hand at a simple landscape featuring one or two dwarf conifers, combined with rocks, driftwood, moss or baby tears, perhaps with an accessory such as a miniature bridge or a house in an appropriate scene, Plate 38. Later, you can develop many kinds of natural scenes. For a garden club member studying landscape design, you might copy in small scale a Japanese garden, with tiny oriental bridges, wet peatmoss molded with a fork into the shape of mountains, pebbles for outlining a beach and white sand to simulate waves. A woodland can be planted with moss and ferns, a patio garden in the old Spanish style can hold tiny clay pots and tiny tesserae tiles. Trellises, pools, boats and other ornaments can be bought at the dime store. Fences, retaining walls, garden houses, sundials, bird baths, benches and seats of stone, wood or concrete all will give realism to an outdoor scene and are easily made from small materials.

In designing your miniature garden, consider also the paths which must lead from one point to another. They may be of grass, tanbark, or constructed of stepping stones of wood or flagstone. The grading of the landscape is another consideration: hills and slopes add to the picture.

Big or little, a landscape should have a center of interest, be harmonious in texture and color, and have a good relationship of all parts to each other as well as to the whole design.

The focal point or center of interest should dominate the scene. This may be a tree, or perhaps a garden feature such as a pool or a well. Build up the attraction by creating paths or open lawn to frame it. Framing the center of interest with plants will also draw the eye to it.

The container may be concrete, wood, or ceramic, depending on its intended placement. The one in Plate 39 fits neatly into a window garden. Drainage holes should be covered first with screening, then with a layer of pebbles. Add some charcoal, about 1″ of soil (or more) and then the plants. Sprinkle soil over the roots and tamp it down before watering. An all-purpose soil mixture is 2 parts coarse sand, 1 part leaf mold and 1 part garden loam.

To water the dish garden in a ceramic container, immerse the container in water *almost* but not quite reaching the top. Let stand until the soil feels wet to the touch. Containers that cannot be immersed in water must be sprinkled from the top, as carefully as possible to avoid upsetting any of the garden features.

MAKING A TERRARIUM

A small garden under glass with its own glass cover—actually a miniature greenhouse—is a charming and unusual gift for anyone who is interested in nature study. It is an interesting feature for any room, usually it becomes the main attraction and a decorative center or interest. A terrarium seems to have universal appeal.

It should be planted with young plants of whatever kind are used. Packaged plant materials for terraria are available from many sources, or you can use peperomia, fern, dwarf English ivy, boxwood, dracaena, croton, begonias, violets, anemones, and pelargonium, among many others.

Glass globes from floral supply houses, large brandy snifters, fishbowls, candy jars, square sided mason jars or the conventional rectangular Wardian case are available.

Plate 39   A dish garden is universally popular. This uses variegated sansevieria for height, Chinese fern, variegated aucuba and smaller varieties of sansevieria and draecena. The driftwood and grey ceramic birds add to the atmosphere and grey-green color of the plant material and container.
Arranged by Mrs. Joe E. Wolff   *(Photo by Joe E. Wolff)*

Plate 40   A large brandy snifter is a container for grey and green succulents with rocks and sand to complete a desert landscape.   *(Photo Steve James)*

You may start by lining the container with pieces of moss packed close together, the green part facing the glass. To provide drainage (a necessity since there are no drainage holes) add a layer of pebbles, then a handful of charcoal. If you are not using moss, the layer of pebbles comes first. Then add top soil or a mixture of 2 parts coarse sand, 1 part leaf mold or peat moss, and 2 parts garden loam.

The soil can be shaped into little slopes and valleys, with large stones for craggy mountains and small pebbles to simulate a path.

Now plant the growing things; lay on more moss for sod or more soil. Spray half a cup of water over the surface, wipe glass and put on the cover, which must be lifted whenever the garden is too moist.

With your gift of a miniature garden, be sure to include a list of plant material with the following directions:

1. Whenever water or mold collect in the terrarium, lift off or tilt the cover until the soil and glass dry.

2. Water moderately when necessary—not more than half a cup at a time so water does not collect around the roots. Watering every two weeks will probably be ample—once every two months may be enough.

3. If the terrarium is made from cacti and succulents, as in Plate 40, the cover should always remain partly open so that there is air space at all times. It is also possible to use without a cover and water occasionally as needed.

6

fragrancies: old-fashioned gifts

Fragrance, like music, is memory making. The smell of a spring day, the scent of lilacs, an old-fashioned rose—all of these can evoke remembrances of another day long past and all but forgotten. To create sweet memories for your own family, why not plan your own garden with scent in mind? Annuals such as carnations, heliotrope, mignonette, nicotiana, stock, and sweet peas; perennials such as sweet violets, and lily of the valley; hyacinth and tuberose bulbs; honeysuckle and sweetpea vines, and a host of fragrant shrubs including the lilacs, mock-orange, and roses . . . here are gifts of fragrance your children will enjoy forever in remembrance if not in reality.

With a supply of scented plant material, your presents can recapture old-fashioned pleasures. Acquaint your friends with the subtleties of a pomander ball in the closet, a rose jar in the living room (opened a moment before company arrives), and sachets among the linens and lingerie. From Japan, introduce the custom of putting favorite fragrant herbs underneath the welcome mat at the front door. As callers step on the mat, the crushed herbs release their aromas.

You may add fragrance to homemade candles, soap, ink and cosmetics; put a rose or geranium petal in your stationery box, in letters, and between the pages of books. Fragrance is a lovely tradition in bureau drawers and linen closets, in the fireplace, in laundry rinse water and in starch. Consider fragrance when you are arranging flowers and corsages to give.

DRYING ROSE AND OTHER FLOWER PETALS
Pick the flowers in the morning after the dew is dried, but before the sun is at its height.

Dry the petals on newspapers, blotters, large wire screens, or shelves of netting or canvas in a cool, airy, shady place. You may also dry whole petals in sand.

Once the petals are dried, they may be left whole and packed loosely or rubbed to a powder. Store in airtight containers. Dried petals put into a tea pot release a refreshing fragrance.

ROSE CONCENTRATES

There are a number of ways to obtain a concentrated essence of rose for use in making perfumes:

1. A simple one for a patient gardener is oil of roses. Fill a quart jar three-quarters full with fresh, fragrant rose petals. Cover the rose petals with either olive or sesame oil, put on the lid and place in the sun for forty days. Strain.

2. For this one you will need a wooden bucket or container. Fill it three-quarters full with fresh, fragrant roses; cover them with pure water, and put in the sun. When the oil rises to the surface, collect it with absorbent cotton, and squeeze it into a bottle.

A variation of this method is to substitute rosewater for the petals and water, leave it out all night in a large, open container, and then skim off the oil in the morning.

3. This method will take six weeks, and you will need a crock or earthen jar with a tight cover. Alternate a layer of fresh, fragrant rose petals with a layer of coarse salt. Repeat this until the container is full, and then cover tightly.

Let stand undisturbed in a cool, dark spot for six weeks to purify. One drop of this essence is so concentrated that it is guaranteed to perfume a pint of water.

4. Another concentrate of roses which will last for years is made with fresh fragrant rose petals and a dry white wine such as sauterne. Put the petals in a bottle, cover them with the wine, and keep the bottle tightly closed.

ROSE PERFUME

Once you have the oil of roses you can make perfume. Take one ounce of the fragrant rose oil, dissolve it in 20 ounces of rubbing alcohol, and add 5 ounces of water.

ROSE WATER

Rose water is the basis for many of the fragrancies; it has varied uses in cooking. Sprinkle rose water on the ironing board for fragrant lingerie; put it in an atomizer and spray electric light bulbs with it—only when they are turned off, of course With your gift of rose water, include a list of its possible uses.

The simplest recipe for making rose water is this: Wash carefully two pounds of fragrant red rose petals, and remove the bitter white or green base. Put petals in an earthenware container and cover with rainwater.

Slowly bring almost to the boil; then let it cool before straining and bottling.

If you remember your high-school chemistry you might like to try this method for *distilling* rose water: Fill a metal coffee pot half-full with rose petals and rain water. Cover tightly and attach a rubber hose to the spout at one end with the other end of the hose in a glass bottle on the floor.

Put a basin of cold water on the floor, and rest part of the hose in it.

Heat the petals and water slowly. The vapors will pass through the hose, becoming condensed as they go through the cold water, and thus reaching the glass jar as rose water.

GIFTS OF FRAGRANT COSMETICS

Long before cosmetics were sold, women experimented at home with such materials as cucumbers, oatmeal, almonds, lemons, honey, buttermilk, rose water, rice flour, olive oil, lard, and even strawberries. Homemade cosmetics may never replace Helena Rubinstein's brand, but they are fun to experiment with, and a unique gift for the woman who "has everything." If she is allergic to some of the chemicals used in commercial cosmetics, the person who receives your brand of beauty aid may be forever grateful!

FRAGRANT SOAP

> 1 bar castille or white unperfumed soap
> 6 ounces rose water
> 1 teaspoon dried rose petals
> ½ teaspoon dried lavender flowers
> ¼ teaspoon each dried thyme and rosemary

Cut the bar of soap into small chips, and dissolve in hot rose water. Beat the dried rose petals and herbs together in a mortar until finely pulverized. Add them to the soap and rose water mixture. Pour into a mold such as an ashtray, coaster, gelatin mold, or a milk carton.

To make a shampoo or a liquid soap, dissolve the soap in more rose water and bottle attractively.

FACIALS

Powdered buttermilk mixed with finely pulverized rose petals in an apothecary jar makes a very special gift. It may be added to the bath, or to the water when face washing, or make it into a thick paste for a facial. I found an instant powdered buttermilk at the supermarket which I use for this.

For another effective facial, add rose water to a warm, pure honey, or you may substitute finely pulverized rose petals for the rose water.

CREAMS AND LOTIONS

Using instant buttermilk again, make a *lotion* by mixing 2 ounces of the buttermilk powder and 1 tablespoon of soy oil to every 8 ounces of rose water.

As an emollient or *lubricant* for the skin and hair, mix 1 teaspoon of pulverized rose petals to every 4 ounces of lanolin. Instead of the lanolin you might also try coco butter or coconut oil which many California suntanners swear by.

An uncomplicated but refreshing *skin cream* may be made from rose water, soy oil, and gelatin.

> 1 tablespoon gelatin
> ½ cup water
> 6 ounces rose water
> 3 tablespoons soy oil

Combine gelatin and water, and let soften for five minutes. Simmer until dissolved, and add to rose water and oil. Mix thoroughly, and chill.

SKIN FRESHENERS

> 12 ounces witch hazel
> 2 ounces dried rose petals
> 1 ounce dried lavender
> leaves and flowers
> ½ ounce dried mint
> ½ ounce dried rosemary

Fill a pint jar with the herbs and witch hazel. Cover tightly and leave at room temperature for about two weeks, shaking the bottle occasionally. Strain and bottle.

Other herbs that you might use singly or in combination for skin fresheners are lemon balm, lemon verbena, rose geranium leaves, sweet basil, sweet marjoram, and thyme.

HAIR RINSES

Other fragrant herbs and flowers may substitute for or combine with rose petals in this very simple recipe. Fill a jar half full of rose petals and cover with white wine vinegar. Set in the sun for one or two days, strain, and bottle.

Collect rainwater to use as the soft-water base for the following two hair rinses. For the first rinse, simply soak ½ cup of dried rose petals in every pint of rain water for 24 hours; strain.

The second rinse uses ½ cup of either rosemary or lemon verbena—plus ¼ cup camomile flowers if the rinse is intended for a blonde. Simmer the herbs for half an hour in 24 ounces of rain water; strain and bottle.

HAIR LACQUER

Slice two lemons and cover with a cup of rose water. Boil until the juice of the lemons has been extracted; strain and bottle.

BATH SACHETS

To make a bath a more luxurious and refreshing affair, make little sachets of crushed scented herbs in muslin or silk bags tied with a long ribbon to be hung on the faucet and used repeatedly.

The sachet may be infused in boiling water for ten minutes or put directly into the bath. For gifts, either bottle the infusion, or give the sachets in little boxes with directions for use.

My favorite blend for bath sachets has equal parts of dried rose petals, lavender, lemon balm, and lemon verbena. Other blends might include chamomile, lemon peel, mints, jasmine, orange flowers, rose geranium leaves, rosemary, thyme, sage, and woodruff.

POTPOURRIS

Potpourris, sweet bags and sachets, pillows and pomanders can all contribute to the atmosphere of a house and give it a definite character. They are charming gifts which, if presented as an *ensemble* of matched fragrances, can be quite appropriate even where you want more than a "little" gift.

Almost everyone who knows about potpourri has a favorite recipe, copied, perhaps, from a quaint old book, or inherited from grandmother, or possibly passed along by another member of your garden club. The simplest formula is to fill a jar about three-quarters full, alternating ½ inch of dried fragrant petals with 1 tablespoon of salt.

After this, just about any fragrance can be added. Here is my favorite potpourri recipe:

16 ounces dried rose petals
10 ounces dried fragrant flowers: lavender, carnations, sweet peas, violets, lily-of-the-valley
2 ounces each dried marjoram, lemon thyme, and rosemary
1 tablespoon orris root
1 teaspoon each allspice, cloves, and pulverized bay leaves
2 teaspoons dried chopped lemon and orange peel

Mix ingredients thoroughly and put in an airtight container. Let mellow for 6 weeks, stirring occasionally. The potpourri can then be transferred to smaller containers for gift giving.

Because scent is such an individual thing, you will undoubtedly want to do some of your own experimenting. Here is the basic recipe which you can use as a guide:

2 quarts of flowers and herbs which dry to one quart.

Flowers: buddleia, carnation, heliotrope, honeysuckle, jasmine, lily of the valley, magnolia, mignonette, orange flowers, rose, rose geranium, stock, sweet pea, violet.

Herbs: angelica root, ambrosia, anise, basil, bay, caraway, cardamon, coriander, hops, lavender, lemon balm, lemon verbena, melilot, marjoram, mints, rosemary, sage, sweet woodruff, thyme, vetiver root.

1 tablespoon of *fixative:* calumus root, gum benzoin, orris root, storax.

1 tablespoon of *spices:* allspice, cinnamon, cloves, ginger, mace, nutmeg, tonka and vanilla beans.

Also a few drops of one or two kinds of oil: bergamot, eucalyptus, heliotrope, jasmine, lavender, lemon verbena, patchouli, peppermint, rhodium, rose geranium, rosemary.

Peels of lemon, orange, tangerine stuck with cloves and cut into small pieces, or dried whole in the oven, and then powder in a mortar.

Cedar and rosewood chips or sawdust; extracts; eau de cologne; glycerine; alcohol; and brandy.

SWEET BAGS AND SACHETS

Any of your favorite potpourri mixtures may be used to fill little bags and pads for linen and bureau drawers, even for stuffing dolls and for padding coat hangers. Make the bags of a fine muslin or mesh fabric folded several times so that the herbs cannot fall out. The bags can be cut from material about 3½ x 12 inches, folded in half crosswise and then seamed along the sides. Fill the bags with the potpourri mixture, and tie with colorful ribbon, to which you may wire a flower or two when the sachets are presented.

For the sachets in Plate 41, Mrs. H. Jefferson Davis gives her recipe as follows:

"Spread rose petals to dry. Treatment is most successful in a warm, dry, dark room. The attic would be excellent.

"For each quart of dried rose petals, use 1 tablespoon each of cloves, cinnamon, allspice, cardomon, rosemary. A few drops of bergamot and rose oils; 1 small jar orris root; small jar red rose sachet; 1 tablespoon whole cloves."

Plate 41 Reminiscent of lavender and old lace are these delicately scented sachets made from rose petals and spices. A "little gift" suitable for many occasions.
Arranged by Mrs. H. Jefferson Davis (Photo B. E. Johnson)

ROSE BEADS OR SACHET BEADS

These beads may be used as sachet for linen and lingerie. If you wish to use them as beads for jewelry, pierce them with a needle when they are dried.

Sprinkle rose petals with salt and run through the meat grinder, using the finest blade. If you have an iron kettle put them in it, or in a bowl with a piece of iron.

As you add new petals, regrind entire mixture. It will begin to work like clay, and will turn jet black. Mold them into beads of the desired shape and size, and ornament them with lines.

Another method is to beat the rose petals with a pestle until you have a thick paste. Roll ½ teaspoon of the paste into a tiny bead and set aside on a screen or tray in a warm, airy spot until the beads are thoroughly dried and hard.

FRAGRANT PILLOWS

Small fragrant pillows to be used between mattresses or placed underneath pillows at night were very popular in past years. Today they make very charming and unusual gifts.

Fill small muslin pillows with potpourri, or with dried sweet-leaved pelargoniums, mints, rose petals, or pine needles. Some combinations you might try are lemon verbena and pine needles; rose geranium and pine needles; rosemary and pine needles; summer savory and pine needles, and lavender and southernwood.

POMANDERS

Gifts of aromatic pomanders or clove balls (Plate 42) are always received with real enthusiasm. It seems that the more sophisticated people are, the more they long for old-fashioned ways. Make pomanders from apples, kumquats, lemons, limes, or oranges. You will also need whole cloves, and spices such as allspice, ground cloves, cinnamon, nutmeg, and orris root powder.

Insert the cloves into the fruit. I put them close enough together so that none of the skin shows. Roll them in orris root or one of the spices, or a blend of them, and dry for about four weeks. To hurry the procedure, you may dry the fruit in a 300° oven for four hours. Place on a shallow pan or heavy aluminum foil.

I use rubber finger guards on thumb and forefinger when making the pomanders since my fingernails turned an oxford gray the first time I made them.

Plate 42 Another old-fashioned gift: pomander balls whose delightful fragrance permeates the room when they are hung from the wall or placed in a bowl upon the table. For maximum preservation, the cloves should cover every part of the fruit. However, these pomanders last well also.

Arranged by Mrs. H. Jefferson Davis

(Photo B. E. Johnson)

When the pomanders are dried, wrap them in cellophane, net, or metallic mesh, and loop a ribbon or wire to them for hanging, or attach to a padded coat hanger.

Making pomander balls is a wonderful activity for children and will keep them busy and happy for hours. Once in desperation I let my 2½ year-old attempt one, after first punching the lemon with holes. He did extremely well inserting the cloves into the holes—and even better taking them out again!

PERFUMED INK

Put a half cup of dried herbs such as lavender, lemon verbena, rose geranium, or rosemary in a saucepan with a little water to cover, and let boil for a few minutes. After it cools, strain. One teaspoon will scent a bottle of ink. If you are really ambitious, and happen to have any pokeberries handy, you could even make your own ink! *Using Wayside Plants* by Nelson Coon (a Hearthside publication) has many such fascinating recipes.

SUGGESTIONS FOR FRAGRANT GIFTS

1. Package seeds of fragrant flowers and herbs in small cellophane or manilla envelopes with cultural directions. Use as greeting cards or package toppers.

2. For a novel sachet, marinate wood chips in flower oils. Samples of rare wood are sometimes available from woodworkers' supply houses and would be ideal for this.

3. Planning a gift of stationery? Buy it a few months before needed, and scent it by putting dried roses or other fragrant flowers in the box.

4. Rose water in a Victorian pitcher with a basin is a charming "gift" for your overnight guest.

5. Pomander balls have many gift uses: top of the package decoration, as a fragrant part of charm strings and wreaths; in a basket by the door as a parting gift to holiday visitors; for making a small, dowel Christmas tree to be used on the entry hall table; to hang from the tree; as table favors; and placed in a bowl on the table.

6. Give a child a sweet-smelling rag or stocking doll stuffed with a sachet or potpourri.

7. Give a coordinated wardrobe of scents: soap, lotion, skin freshener, hair rinse, sweet water, and sachets.

8. To the family of the bride give a basket of dried fragrant rose petals to be tossed at the departing couple. Softer and more fragrant than rice.

9. For the fireplace: boxes of the branches and stems of fragrant herbs such as basil, catnip, hyssop, lemon verbena, marjoram, savory, thyme, and southernwood; or bowls of dried citrus skins cut in strips; or charcoal marinated with essential oils.

7

herbs and other gifts for gastronomes

Culinary herbs such as chives, parsley, marjoram, thyme, fennel, and basil are practically a necessity in any garden planned by gourmets. They are out of the ordinary gifts, and can be presented as potted plants, dried in bunches and put into jars, or frozen in plastic bags. Lemon balm and lemon verbena as well as the mints may be put into little muslin containers for use in brewing herb teas. The aromatic herbs are refreshing, of course, in potpourris, sachets and other fragrances described in Chapter 6.

Herbs are among the easiest of plants to grow. They will do well in average, even poor, soil, need little watering, and in general thrive on neglect. However, good drainage and full sun are important. Herbs are easily included in the garden since one of two plants of each kind will prove more than enough for the family, with surplus for giving. Plant them in a four-feet square border, as an edging or ground cover, or in an old-fashioned knot or herb wheel. But somehow, somewhere, do plant them! Few materials are as rewarding.

HOW TO RAISE HERBS

From Cuttings: In the spring, cut a shoot about three inches long from last year's plant. Strip the leaves from the bottom, then plant the cutting in light soil which has good drainage. Spray for several days, especially in warm weather, until the plant is established. The cutting may also be put into a peat pot for immediate giving.

Some herbs produce little roots all along their stem—plant these just as you do the cuttings. Among the herbs which can be propagated by cuttings or rooting stems are balm, lavender, pot marjoram, rosemary, the mints, sage, and thyme.

Seeds: If you are patient and thrifty, you might wish to start herbs from seeds. Annuals such as basil, summer savory, parsley, chervil and caraway can be put into the garden in the Spring, right where they are to grow, or started indoors in peat pots, to be planted outdoors in the garden later. They can also be sown in a sunny window box. One disadvantage:

seeds such as parsley germinate slowly—as much as two months are needed
—so it is best to buy plants.

Seeds should always be sown in rows, and thinned as soon as the seedlings can be handled, leaving only the strongest. Be sure to label the rows.

Care: Plant annual and perennial herbs in separate beds. The annual
bed should be dug up each year, but the perennials need only to be cultivated and covered with leaves in the winter. Keep weeds out of both beds
since they compete with the plants for food. Herbs need watering only
when they are newly planted, or in an exceptionally dry spell but they do
require full sun and good drainage.

In Window Boxes or Pots: Many herbs can be grown indoors. Parsley,
chives, rosemary and thyme are a good beginning (Figure 22A). Sweet
marjoram or a scented geranium could be substituted for the parsley which,
although very popular, is so easy to buy. Plant them indoors in window
box or clay pot—even cigar boxes—and trim plants as necessary to maintain their good shape. The trimmed leaves become part of your gift stockpile.

HOW TO HARVEST HERBS

Not all parts of the herb plant are useful, so it is important to know *what*
to harvest before you decide how. The alphabetical list later in this chapter should be consulted. Where the flower is needed—as in making wine
or for decoration—cut perfect blossoms before the flower is fully open. To
collect seed, hang flowers upside down, then tie a paper or freezer bag
over them. Seeds will drop into the bag to be used for next year's supply
of gifts, or for immediate giving. In either case, be sure to keep plant seeds
separated by kind, and clearly labeled. Leaves can be taken at any time,
but leave enough for plant growth. In cutting the stem itself, take only
enough for immediate use. Before winter, many herbs—for instance rosemary, basil, chives and thyme—can be potted up and moved indoors to
supply plants for winter giving. For a friend's kitchen, paint some clay pots
with enamel in matching colors, and fill with potted herbs. Be sure to include some of your favorite recipes for cooking and potpourris.

HOW TO DRY HERBS

Method 1: Tie them loosely in small bunches and hang from cord in an
airy closet or attic (Fig. 22B). When dry, strip off coarse stems and store
leaves in airtight jars, or cellophane envelopes, labelled properly, since dry
herbs look pretty much alike.

Method 2: Strip leaves from stems. Arrange leaves one layer deep in a
shallow cardboard box or on a screen. Let dry in airy attic or porch. Label
boxes. Herbs deteriorate quickly so should be dried as soon after gather-
ing as possible. When stems are brittle, the herbs are dry. Single envelopes
with fragrant dry herbs may be stapled to a gift card.

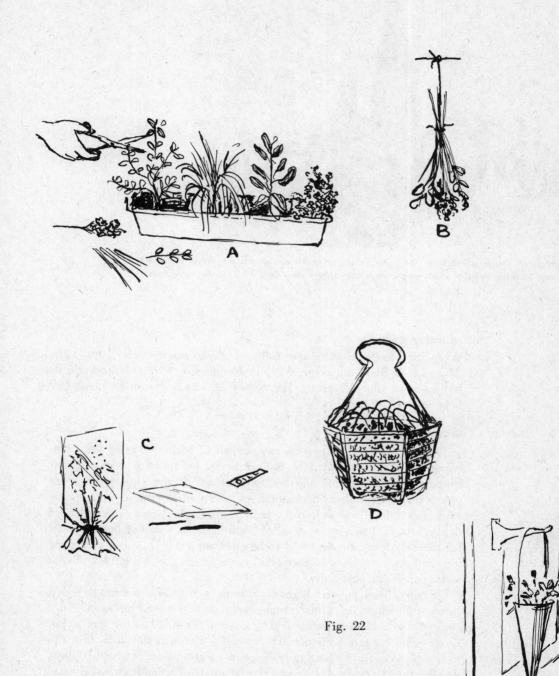

Fig. 22

Plate 43 Herb vinegars are very easy to concoct and make attractive gifts in containers such as these, many of which have been salvaged after other uses. *(Photo Steve James)*

TO FREEZE HERBS

Wrap fresh herbs in aluminum foil or put into small freezer bags. (Fig. 22C). Label. Store in freezer. Wrap in average-size servings since herbs do not last well after defrosting. Herbs may also be frozen in bouquets (see below).

HERB RECIPES

Teas are delicious made from any number of herbs including the mints, borage, camomile, dill, fennel, juniper berry, lemon balm, lemon thyme, lemon verbena, mistletoe, parsley, sweet woodruff and parsley. Give one or a blend of these dried herbs, perhaps with a silver strainer or tea cosy, or wrapped in cheesecloth bags. Include directions: Steep one teaspoon dried herbs or 1 tablespoon crushed fresh herbs in a cup of boiling water for three or four minutes. Said to be good for colds . . . and *very* good iced and sent over in a pitcher to a neighbor busy in his garden. Try it with peppermint next July.

Vinegars. Most popular herbs for vinegars are basil, burnet, caraway, chives, dill, lemon balm, marjoram, rosemary, thyme and tarragon. Put 2 cups of fresh, bruised herbs or 1½ tablespoons dried herbs into a jar. Cover with 1 quart boiling cider or white, wine vinegar, to within two inches of top of jar. Cover tightly. Keep in a warm place for about 10 days, shaking the jar every day or so. Save attractive bottles from soda, salad dressings, and other supermarket items (Plate 43) to carry your gift.

Herb Bouquets. Bouquets of herbs or *bouquet garni* are not on the market, but they are necessary seasonings for most French sauces, stews, soups, court bouillons, fish fumets, etc. Friends who are gourmets would be delighted to get a quantity of these made up for use. The bouquets can be frozen.

Tie 4 sprigs of parsley, 2 sprigs each of thymeand tarragon and a small bay leaf in cheesecloth about 3 inches square. The bouquet is removed before the dish is served. Try it in your own kitchen as your gift to the family.

Herbs are perfectly paired with one of those enchanting little French parsley baskets. The basket may be lined with moss and then filled with soil, to carry a potted plant (Fig. 22D). Labelled apothecary jars seem a natural way to present dried herbs.

Herb butters. Marvelous melted over cooked green vegetables, potatoes and scrambled eggs. I like them also over broiled meats and chicken but do not put the herb butter under flame or it will scorch—add to broiled food just before serving. Make up herb butter into little balls and give them to the hostess on the day of the party. They freeze very well too.

Remove stems from fresh herbs—add ¼ cup finely chopped fresh herbs to 4 ounces of butter. Cream well. Add a few drops of lemon juice. Dried herbs can also be used—about 1 teaspoon for each 4 ounces of butter, but mix in fresh green dill or parsley for color. Almost any herb can be used to make herb butter so do experiment.

GUIDE TO HERBS

In giving herbs, mention the dishes which they dramatize and enhance. This list will help.

Balm. Use leaves for flavoring or in tea. Has pronounced lemon flavor.

Basil. Indispensable for tomato and lamb dishes. Good as herb butter. Combines well with tarragon for flounder.

Bay Leaves (Laurel). Leaves may be used green or dried. Pungent flavor can be overpowering; half a leaf may be enough.

Borage. For flavoring sweet drinks; blue flower petals are pretty in lemonade. Try leaves in salad.

Chervil. Something like parsley, but more delicate. Use leaves for flavor and garnish of carrots, eggs, chicken and delicate foods.

Chives. A delicate onion flavor. Can be picked frequently to prevent its flowering.

Coriander. Seeds are dried and used in stuffing, cookies and drinks. Flavor has citrus quality.

Dill. Use the leaves in boiling potatoes or in salads; the seeds pep up eggs and cucumbers. Good in pickling. Try dill sauce with shrimps.

Fennel. Seeds and leaves are good in pies and with poached fish. The stem is used as a vegetable (finocchio).

Lavender. Flowers are used in potpourri or in making lavender bags. Tea made from leaves is reputed to relieve headaches.

Marjoram. Similar to oregano but more subtle. Try leaves of sweet or pot marjoram in green peas, squash, lamb and eggplant, in pot roast and rice.

Mints. Everyone knows about these! Good with peas of course and in making mint sauce and jelly.

Oregano. Indispensable in Italian sauces and stews. Also used in Spanish and Mexican dishes.

Parsley. Probably the world's favorite garnish. Leaves can be dried or frozen and stay green. Use in fish marinades, and most soups and sauces.

Rosemary. The herb which symbolizes remembrance. Perfect with all lamb recipes and in cauliflower with a flavor of thyme or chive added.

Sage. Slightly bitter so use leaves with care. Gives piquant flavor to poultry dressings and pork. Popular in chowders.

Savory. Leaves add flavor to cabbage, turnips and string beans. Summer savory is an annual, winter savory a perennial.

Tarragon. A few leaves go a long way in sauces, but a lot is needed for making tarragon vinegar. Combine with basil for breading veal cutlets. Worthwhile in duck stuffing.

Thyme. Dries well. Delicious in stuffings, stews, tomatoes. Gives pungent flavor to pork and veal.

GARDENING FOR GOURMETS

Crisp bread and butter pickles, mushroom catsups, brandied peaches, shimmering jellies, spiced nuts and delicious fruit butters—how they remind us of grandmother's kitchen and what marvelous gifts they make! They are now easily prepared in our electric stoves, blenders, mixers, pressure cookers and frypans. But alas—gone are the peaches of yesteryear—the mushrooms are tasteless and the strawberries are big in size and small in flavor. Today's fruits and vegetables are picked while still green to make transportation easier. In fact, most commercial varieties are grown only because they travel well; never mind the taste! So if you love good food, it is worth the effort of growing it yourself. The reward comes when you step outside the kitchen door for plump ripe tomatoes, incredibly delicate lettuce leaves, juicy tender corn and tree-ripened fruits.

Gifts of home-grown food are universally popular. Even so simple a present as a basket of ripe apricots, into which you tuck a yellow rose or two (Plate 44) makes a big hit. Look for unusual varieties. Miniatures, always conversation pieces, are especially appealing gifts. There are tiny tomatoes, midget peas, six-inch butternut squash, and other possibilities which require less space than usual varieties, and can be grown even in pocket-size gardens.

Did you know that watercress can be grown on a window sill? Last year, a friend presented a glass planter holding rooted watercress (Fig. 22E) to a couple celebrating their fifteenth (crystal) wedding anniversary. The planter was first filled with water into which was set a bunch of watercress bought in the market. A week or so later there were roots all over the cress. The planter was then half-filled with garden soil and given with a note to keep it filled wth water in an east window. Can you imagine a more delightful gift for a gourmet couple? Inexpensive wide-mouthed jars or fish bowls could replace the hanging vase.

There are so many possibilities for cooked gifts from your garden larder, one hardly knows where to begin. I have chosen only those recipes which are most unusual, most delicious and most attractive—all requirements for gift-giving.

FRUITS, NUTS AND BERRIES

Frosted Fruits. Luncheon hostesses welcome a basket of these. Dip the prettiest fruit into frothy beaten egg white, then into granulated sugar. Dry thoroughly on a rack.

Raspberry Wine. Into an earthen container put 3 cups very ripe raspberries and 1 quart good Rhine wine. Let stand for 2 days. Strain and add two or three ounces of sugar.

Strawberry Wine. Mix 4 quarts crushed strawberries with 1⅓ quarts cold water. Let stand for 24 hours. Strain into a crock. Add 3 pounds granulated sugar, cover crock with a cloth, and put in a dark place for six weeks. Strain and bottle.

Apple-Walnut Jam. Heat 2 cups clover honey, 2 cups apple cider vinegar, 1 teaspoon ground cinnamon, and 1 teaspoon ground cloves. Add 2 pounds chopped apples, and ½ cup chopped walnuts. Boil for 45 minutes, stirring frequently. Pour into hot sterilized jars and seal immediately.

Concord Grape Filling for Tarts
5 cups Concord grapes
   (or any tart variety)
1¼ cups sugar
2 tablespoons quick cooking tapioca
grated rind of 1 lemon
1 tablespoon lemon juice
¼ teaspoon salt
1 tablespoon butter
Slip skins from grapes, saving the skins and placing the pulp in a saucepan. Cook pulp until the seeds loosen, then force through a colander to remove seeds. Return the pulp with the skins to the saucepan and mix in the tapioca, lemon rind, juice and salt. Cook gently for 5 minutes, remove from heat and add butter. Cool slightly. Have tart shells ready (recipe below) on a cookie sheet and fill. Place strips of pastry over filling to form lattice top and bake at 450° F. 10 minutes; reduce heat to 375° F. and continue baking 20 minutes longer. Fills 6 tarts (See Plate 45).

Apple Tart Filling. Peel, core and quarter 2 pounds tart apples, saving the skins. Place skins, 1¼ cups sugar and ½ cup water in saucepan and simmer for 10 minutes or until skins soften. Strain off syrup, discarding the skins. Return syrup to saucepan and add the quartered apples. Cook gently until barely tender. Have unbaked tart shells on a cookie sheet and fill with the apples, draining them slightly. Dust with ½ teaspoon grated nutmeg and dot with butter. Bake in 450 F. oven 10 minutes, then reduce heat to 350° and bake 20 minutes longer. While tarts bake, simmer syrup to about ¾ cup in quantity. Pour over tarts as soon as they are removed from the oven. Serve warm or chilled . . . whipped cream or sour cream tops them deliciously. For 6 tarts (Plate 45).

Plate 45   The beautiful garden-grown fruits of autumn, the squashes, acorns and pumpkins, apples and grapes too, tempt us to bake little tarts promised in advance to our Thanksgiving hostess.   (Photo Courtesy of Reynolds Metals Company)

Tutti-Frutti

Makes a delicious topping for vanilla ice cream, pudding or for preserves if you increase the recipe.

Into a stone jar or crock put one cup good brandy and one cup of ripe
strawberries. Cover with cheesecloth or a soft dishtowel.

As each fruit comes into season, add it at the height of its perfection
with one cup of sugar to each cup of fruit. No more brandy is indicated.
Be sure to stir at each addition. Large fruit should be cut up, cherries and
plums pitted. For a new neighbor as well as a unique shower gift.

FROM THE VEGETABLE GARDEN

Chili Sauce
24 ripe tomatoes
 4 chopped green peppers
 1 pod of red pepper
 1 large minced onion
½ cup of light brown sugar
 2 cups of cider vinegar
 1 teaspoon ground allspice
 1 teaspoon ground cinnamon
 1 teaspoon ground cloves
 1 teaspoon ground ginger
 1 tablespoon salt
Slowly boil the tomatoes, then add peppers, onion, and sugar. Cook until
the mixture thickens.

Add vinegar, spices, and salt, and boil for 10 minutes. Strain and pour
into hot, sterilized jars at once.

Sliced Green Tomato Pickles
6 quarts sliced green tomatoes
1½ quarts onions
salt
2 quarts cider vinegar
2½ pounds brown sugar
1 tablespoon ground cloves
1 tablespoon ground pepper
1 tablespoon allspice
2 tablespoons cinnamon
1 tablespoon celery seed
1 tablespoon mustard seed
Sprinkle tomatoes and onions well with salt. Weight down in colander overnight.

Put spice in bag; bring vinegar and spices to a boil. Add the tomatoes and onions, and boil for 10 minutes, then simmer for 1 hour. Place in hot sterilized jars and seal at once. Nice to prepare for a church potluck supper.

Bread and Butter Pickles
12 medium cucumbers
 6 medium onions
 2 cups vinegar
 1 cup water
½ teaspoon black pepper
 1 teaspoon celery seed
 1 teaspoon mustard seed
 1 teaspoon turmeric powder
 1 cup sugar

Pare and slice cucumber, and slice onions. Soak in salt water for 1½ hours. Drain.

Heat liquid, spices and sugar to a boil. Add vegetables and bring almost to a boil. Pack into hot sterilized jars and seal.

Beet Relish
 2 quarts of diced, cooked beets
 3 small, chopped onions
 3 diced, green peppers
 2 cups of cider vinegar
 2 cups of light brown sugar
½ cup of grated horseradish
 1 tablespoon of salt

Mix all the ingredients, and bring to a boil. Boil for 10 minutes. Pack in hot, sterilized jars and seal at once.

Pickled Beets
 3 pounds of beets
 2 cups of cider vinegar
½ cup of water
½ cup of sugar
 1 stick cinnamon
 1 teaspoon whole allspice
 6 whole cloves
 1 teaspoon mace
 1 bay leaf

Boil beets, and remove skins. If they are small, leave whole; otherwise, slice them.

Put spices into a bag. Bring vinegar, water, sugar, and spices to a boil. Add beets, and boil for 5 minutes. Pack in hot sterilized jars, and fill with hot liquid. Seal at once.

COOKING WITH FLOWERS

"Garden flowers were domesticated for their medicinal properties and to please the gourmet's palate long before they were grown for their beauty and fragrance. The gentle art of flower cookery . . . is gaining enthusiasts in the United States. Blossoms are being squeezed, chopped, dried, stewed, boiled and baked into seasonings, salads, sandwiches, stews, pies, wines, liquors, teas, jams and jellies." So reads a recent article in *Montana Gardens*. Certainly there never has been so much interest in cooking with flowers and herbs. A recent book on the subject, *Using Wayside Plants* by Nelson Coon (published by Hearthside Press) gives many ideas for cooking wild plants in extraordinary ways. Included are recipes for making blueberry bread, dandelion wine, rose hip jam, and many other wildlings.

Edible Flowers. Have you ever tasted flowers? Rose geranium leaves or rose petals, for instance, may be used in pound cake, baked pears, fruit compote, ice cream, sauce, cake frostings, rice, custard and pudding. Nasturtium, called Indian watercress, is an edible and attractive garnish. According to the *West Virgina Garden News*, ½ cup nasturtium stems, chopped, are added to former President Eisenhower's vegetable soup. Pot marigold leaves add a salty flavor to salads. And violets, according to Venetians, are considered a tasty addition to salads.

Candied Flowers. Use rose petals, violets, sweet peas, borage flowers, mint leaves, or orange blossoms. Dip the flowers or leaves into egg white (or use a small brush) coating both sides. Then cover with granulated sugar. Dry thoroughly on rack. Arrange attractively and give as decoration for bridal, graduation, or birthday cakes.

Flower Sandwiches. Give this to the garden club ladies at a tea. Use homemade brown bread thinly sliced and spread with sweet butter. For the filling you have a choice of chopped marigolds, geranium leaves, nasturtiums, rose petals, or violets. The petals must be carefully washed of course.

Rose Petal Conserve. Blanch 1 pound of rose petals by quickly dipping them into boiling water. Bring 2 tablespoons orange juice, ⅔ cup water and 2 cups sugar to a boil. When sugar is dissolved, add rose petals. Simmer until mixture thickens. Pack into hot sterilized jars and seal.

Garnishes. Try fresh cowslips on breakfast cereal; blue borage for salad decoration. Freeze small flowers in ice cubes to accompany summery drinks. Arrange leaves—mint or any of the scented geraniums—in a lemon gelatin mold, add a thin coating of gelatin, and let this set before adding the rest of the gelatin. Pretty and refreshing. Stuff tulips from which the pistils have been removed with tuna fish salad. Don't overlook any of the decorative possibilities of garden flowers and leaves.

8

garden gifts for children

In one way or another, most of the gift projects in this book can be adapted by children or for them. Pomanders, sachets, rooted geraniums in water, home-propagated succulents, glycerinized leaves, potpourris, seed mosaics in heart and wreath shapes, and miniature arrangements—all of them appeal to youngsters. But some garden projects bring a special glow to the child's face because they are so well suited to his abilities and interests. First on the list must go the growing of plants from familiar foods—suddenly a whole new world seems to open to him! How exciting is the miracle of propagation as it unfolds to the eyes of the youngster for the first time!

PLANTS FROM ORDINARY FRUITS AND VEGETABLES

Fun for children to do, they also make attractive house plants. Encourage your youngster to grow them as a gift for mother and grandmother on Mother's Day, to carry to school, and for young friends on occasions when a thoughtful little present is needed.

Avocado Tree. Put one end of the seed in water suspended by four toothpicks over edge of glass jar. Transplant into small pot holding planting soil when roots are two or three inches long. In 7 or 8 months there will be an exotic looking, treelike plant. If leaves fall off in winter, they will grow back in spring.

Carrot Top Fern. Cut a 1½" slice from the top of the carrot, including some of the stem. Put the flat part in a little dish with ½" of water or moist pebbles. In about a week, fernlike leaves will begin to show. Plant a few carrots in a row for best effect. Carrot plants last a few months.

Dates. Plant 8 pits in a 5-inch pot, just barely covering them with good potting soil. A small, tropical, looking, palmlike plant will be grown in about a year.

Orange, Lemon and Grapefruit Seeds. Plant 8 seeds in a 4" pot containing good potting soil. Cover with another ½-inch of soil. The plant will grow several inches the first year.

112

Plate 46   Planting an indoor "vegetable garden"—tops of carrots, turnips, beets, onions from the grocer. Insert the vegetable tops in soil (in an indoor flat, or cherry crate) so that the sprouts or "crown" are exposed, the remainder buried.   (Photo Bernice Brilmayer)

Peach Pit. Plant one in soil 1-inch down. A lovely unusual plant will grow in 2 or 3 months.

Pineapple-Top Bromeliad. Slice off the leafy top of the pineapple, remove fruit pulp and put the top into water to root. The plant will last for years in water. It does not need direct sunlight.

Sweet-Potato Vine. Put ⅓ of the sweet potato in water, suspending the narrow end in water held by four toothpicks. The heart-shaped vines grow indefinitely in water. Help growth along with plant food and a bit of charcoal. In a year or so, the plant may grow five or six feet tall.

With the exception of pineapple, all of these plants need some sunlight and water.

A GARDEN IN THE WINDOW

Plates 46, 47 and 48 illustrate the growth of a vegetable garden planted in a wooden flat, for a wide window sill in a child's room, where he can intimately observe how it grows, and be given the responsibility for its watering. Teach your child to feel the soil daily; when it feels dry, show him how to sprinkle it with his watering can. In repaying him with pleasure, satisfaction, and self confidence as his plants mature, is there a gift—no matter how costly—which can do as much?

Plate 47 Make sure the vegetable garden never dries out, but don't keep soil soggy wet and muddy. Feel the soil; if it feels dry and crumbly, water carefully; if not, wait until soil is dry.   *(Photo Bernice Brilmayer)*

Plate 48   Less than one month after planting, the vegetables are growing well: Top, carrot and beet; front, turnip and onion.   *(Photo Bernice Brilmayer)*

FUN WITH GOURDS

For the youngster with time on his hands provide a gift of gourd seeds to be grown in the summer. In the Fall he can devote his extra hours to curing and preserving gourds, making Christmas presents for friends from this bounty. A table on the sidewalk in September, offering gourds instead of lemonade for sale, might make him a real money-maker!

On a quiet day at summer's end, invite the neighbors' children over and help them carve dolls from gourds, to be used as bedroom doorstops. Children are always amused by caricatures of birds and animals fashioned from gourds. Birdhouses and cricket cages (complete with cricket) will fascinate youngsters who are interested in nature.

JELLY APPLES

A Halloween treat for the tricksters who ring your bell. Wash and dry 6 apples and insert wood skewers into them. In top of double boiler, combine 1 cup of sugar, 4 tablespoons light corn sirup, ½ cup water. Cook until sugar is dissolved. Using a candy thermometer, slowly bring temperature to 300° F. Set pan into boiling water placed over bottom of double boiler, add a few drops of red vegetable coloring and dip apples on skewers into the sirup. Turn each apple quickly so it is covered evenly and smoothly. Put the skewers into a rack to cool. The rack of a broiling pan will do nicely. The candy gets hard if left overnight.

FRIENDSHIP BRANCH MOBILE AND TREES

The friendship branch mobile (A) derives from a Japanese custom of wishing good fortune and prosperity to one's friends. It is made from a bare branch at least one foot long, with a couple of twigs extended on each side, near the end. Suspended from it may be fresh or dried flowers, charms, pine cones, or ornaments which have particular significance for

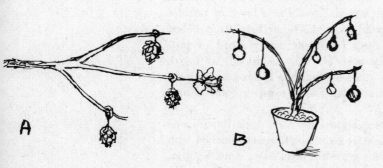

Fig. 23

the friend. The branches may be plain, gilded or painted with glue and glitter, and the little ornaments are wired into place. However they are prepared, isn't this a charming little gift for a friend before he leaves for summer camp?

The money tree (B) fascinates youngsters. Find an interesting bare branch and plunge it upright into a colorful container holding styrofoam. Heavy branches may be held with plaster of Paris. Put a layer of pebbles or tiny Christmas balls on top. Suspend from the limbs brightly polished copper pennies attached with jump rings (from the hobby shop) or fastened to strings with floral clay. The branches may be gilded, whitened, sprayed with paint, or covered with glued-on sequins. Instead of the pennies you may have little seed pods, sea shells, Easter eggs, or colorful hair ribbons.

The snowman tree, Plate 49, was designed by Mrs. Jack Rardin one Christmas. The driftwood and plaque were painted white and touched with glitter to represent snow. The snowmen are white with black hats, buttons, arms and eyes. Their scarves and noses are red, as are the Christmas balls. The eggshells with snowmen inside are sprayed gold. Pfitzer juniper and yew were the evergreens. Wouldn't your youngsters enjoy such a tree this Christmas?

The topiary tree in Plate 50 is a variation of the one shown in Plate 9 and is made the same way. However, this one is adapted for a child by inserting a second, smaller ball of Oasis onto the dowel, covering with chicken wire, and filling with clippings from boxwood. Tiny toys and small ornaments fill in the spaces. They can be wired or stuck in with hairpins or toothpicks. Such a tree would be appealing for Chanukah, when it is customary to give a series of little presents for each successive holiday night. A child will delight in it during Advent, the period which covers the four Sundays before Christmas. Children hang ornaments on the tree each night, making a little ceremony of the pre-holiday season.

Plate 50   This topiary tree makes a charming and welcome gift for a child when it is adapted to his interest by decorating it with tiny toys and miniature ornaments.
Arranged by Mrs. H. Jefferson Davis   (Photo B. E. Johnson)

9

the art of attractive presentation

Particularly with homemade or home-grown gifts, the wrapping is a very important part of the presentation. Unless the wrapping is careful and imaginative, the present will seem *too* casual and unplanned . . . perhaps a little tacky. On the other hand, appropriate wrapping will add a quality of formality and sophistication even to a little gift.

Gift wrapping requires practice and imagination . . . and just as important, a cubbyhole for storing needed equipment. Cellophane, Saran wrap, aluminum foil, paper doilies, and ribbons, cords and rickrack in variety are useful. Boxes of different sizes, Scotch tape, seals, wire, mailing equipment and cards are all vital. Mailing equipment should include sturdy boxes, corrugated paper, excelsior, heavy wrapping paper, string, brown tape, and labels.

Don't be afraid to use color. Try gift wraps done with different shades of blue and green; with violet, orange and pink; with pink and red; simple gold and white or silver and green.

BOXES AND BASKETS

Save last year's Christmas boxes, and make them new again by wrapping the lid and the bottom separately in decorative wrapping paper. With con-tact paper, cover square and rectangular boxes from department stores, milk cartons and cake, cereal and detergent boxes. Tin cans and flower pots may also be covered with Con-tact paper and used as containers. Be on the lookout throughout the whole year for unusually shaped bottles and pottery, wooden boxes, and flowered tins to house your gifts.

And baskets—an ideal way to "box" a gift and an extra gift in itself, Plate 51. There are many types to choose from and they serve many functions, especially for gifts from the garden. Line a basket with heavy aluminum foil and use it as a planter or to carry a huge bouquet of flowers to a friend. For a note of whimsy attach butterflies or birds to the handle with Scotch-tape.

Baskets may be filled with fruit, vegetables, gourds, or evergreens, or a combination basket including separately wrapped packages of nuts, preserves, and jellies. These latter are fun to make up and a joy to receive—a wonderful gift for a whole family. A luxuriously wide, colorful bow adds to the decoration.

Make clay pots more attractive by painting them with enamel paint (it does not peel off as flat paint does). Pots may be decorated with mosaic tiles, pebbles, even sea shells. To mosaic a clay pot, affix the ceramic tile, pebbles, or sea shells with ceramic-tile adhesive which is waterproof. When you have covered the pot with the mosaic, use a rubber spatula to fill in the cracks with grout. After a few minutes wipe off surface with a slightly dampened cloth.

THE BEAUTIFUL BOW

A beautiful bow identifies the professionally wrapped package, and even those of us who are all thumbs (green or otherwise), may learn to make a proper one, Fig. 24.

Plate 51   This pretty basket could decorate a table or mantel at Christmas. It holds a simple grouping of fir, cones and clusters of gilded dates.

(Photo Jeannette Grossman)

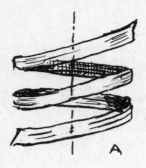

A

B

Fig. 24

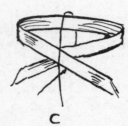

C

D

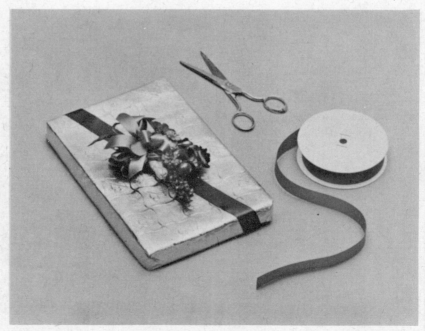

Plate 52 A dried corsage makes a lovely topping for a package and is an extra long-lasting gift.
(Photo Jeannette Grossman)

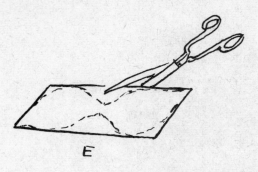

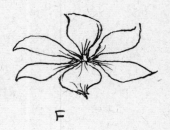

E   F

Start by becoming "bow conscious": examine carefully the bows that you like and soon you will get a feeling for their construction. Here are three of the principal "secrets" for making them:

1. Rather than using one piece of ribbon for tying the package and for making the bow, always use two different ones. Attach the bow to the tying ribbon with a spot of glue or wire.

2. To insure good proportion, remember that the narrower the ribbon, the shorter the loop of the bow should be.

3. Do not knot your bows; tie the center separately with a pieces of wire or thread.

GREETING CARDS

Decorating your own greeting cards with garden materials can be fun for the family to do together. People always seem to look forward to receiving the home-made variety, because such cards have individuality.

Here are some ideas to try:

1. A sprig of holly or evergreen taped to a card and tied with a tiny bow.

2. Sachets or packets of rare seeds or herbs on a card.

3. A pomander ball with a greeting attached.

4. A Christmas tree ball of decorated styrofoam.

5. A tiny corsage of holly or pine cones and seed pods.

6. A dried miniature flower protected by Saran Wrap as the basis for a card.

7. For the youngster, a sachet shaped like a Christmas tree.

8. Fabric cards made with a seed design; these could be framed.

9. Photographs of your garden, leaf forms or wreaths; photograms.

10. With a big bunch of flowers, give the attractive *Home and Garden Calendar* which Hearthside puts out every year at a dollar.

11. Bookmarks fade from pressed miniature flowers and Saran Wrap, or with flowers encased in tiny plastic discs suspended from ribbons or cords.

12. Tiny wreaths made from seeds on a cork background.

Plate 53   For gift plants, aluminum foil and printed gift tape make an unusual and gay package. Tie with ribbons and small Christmas balls.   *(Photo Courtesy Reynolds Wrap)*

DECORATING AND PACKAGING IDEAS

Decorate packages with cut-outs from seed catalogs and packets of seeds.

Top your gift with a corsage of dried materials, or small pine cones and seed pods, or fresh or artificial flowers, or succulents, Plate 53.

Press some leaves. Wrap package in white shelf or tissue paper; attach leaves with a spot of glue and cover all with Saran Wrap.

For gifts with a fragrance, store sachets in with your gift wrappings. Attach a pomander ball, a sachet, (25B) or a molded bar of soap, or follow an old Swedish custom and wrap your gifts in pine boughs.

Fresh Flowers. When taking flowers to friends, dampen the stems and wrap them in a piece of aluminum foil or plastic. They will hold in the moisture and cling to the flowers without need for rubber bands or string, which cut off circulation in the stems.

Fig. 25

Corsages. Wrap them in milk cartons which have been covered with self-adhering paper. Tie a tiny corsage to the top of the package. Dried corsages make handsome decorations for any packages.

Plaques and Pictures. Decorate the box with corsages made from the materials used in the gift.

Potted Plants. Wrap them in aluminum foil and decorate the edges with printed Christmas gift tape. Tie with ribbons and small Christmas balls (Plate 53).

A bought gift can be made more personal with decorations made from natural materials. It's fun to relate the wrappings to the gift itself, Fig. 25. For a fisherman, gild or paint starfish, sea horses and sand dollars and glue them to the package or secure with a dab of floral clay. A gift of towels or sheets in a rose pattern can be decorated with a well-conditioned rose at the top of the package. On a package containing a handsome kitchen gift tie a small flat branch to the outside and wire dime store measuring spoons to the twigs. Draw an umbrella and paste flowers to its shape on a package containing a shower gift. And for an ensemble effect, harmonize your greeting card to the overall package.

index

Japanese
  garden, 86
  maple, 70
  quince, 70
  trees, 74
Jasmine, 93, 94
Jellies, 119
Jelly apples, 115
Jewelry, 46, 96
Joe-pye-weed, 20
Jonquil, 10
July, 11
June, 11
Juniper, 78, 85, 102, 116

K

Kangaroo vine, 58
Kelp, 49
Kengai bonsai, 74
Kerrybush, 70
Key rings, 55
Kumquats, 96

L

Labeling of bulbs, 69
Lagenaria, 52
Laminating, 55, 56
Lamps, 52
Landscape, 10, 85, 88
Larkspur, 11
Latch wiring, 81, 83
Laurel, 31, 41
Lavender, 92, 93, 94, 96, 98, 99, 104
Layering, 58
Leaf
  cuttings, 59, 60
  mold, 63, 73, 76, 88
Leaves, 31, 39, 43, 54
Leis, 10, 33
Lemon
  peel, 93, 94
  seeds, 112
  thyme, 93, 102
  verbena, 92, 93, 94, 96, 98, 99, 102
Lemons, 44, 93, 96
Lentils, 46
Lettuce leaves, 9
Leucothoe, 70
Lichen, 34
Lilac, 70, 89
Lily, 11, 28, 65, 67
Lily-of-the-valley, 10, 11, 89, 93, 94
Limes, 44, 96
Line arrangement, 13, 43
Linen, 89, 94, 96
Lingerie, 90, 96
Long-lasting plant material, 34-54
Lotions, 12, 92, 98
Lotus pods, 40
Lunaria pods, 43

M

Mace, 94
Magnolias, 20, 28, 29, 41, 42, 43, 49, 94
Mailing equipment, 9, 118

Manure tea, 83
Maple, 70, 78
March, 10
Marigolds, 16, 20, 34, 41, 110
Marjoram 92, 93, 94, 98, 99, 100, 102, 104
May Day basket, 11
Melilot, 94
Mignonette, 89, 94
Millet, 42
Mimosa, 11
Miniatures: see individual names
Minima, 85
Mint, 11, 92, 93, 94, 96, 99, 102, 104, 110, 111
Mistletoe, 102
Mobiles, 12, 115-116
Mock-orange, 70, 89
Molds
  for soap, 91
Money tree, 116
Monkey tail, 59
Mosaics, 10, 11, 12, 45, 112, 119
Moss, 82, 86, 88
  stick, 72-73
Mother's Day, 11, 31, 112
Mountain laurel, 70
Mulch, 65
Mullein, 42
Mushrooms, 44

N

Nana, 85
Narcissus, 12, 59, 61, 67
Nasturtiums, 110
New Year, 10
Nicotiana, 89
Nosegay, 25
Notching, 62
Novelties, 26-33
November, 12
Nursery plant material, 58-73
Nutmeg, 94, 96
Nuts, 22, 23, 47, 48, 50, 118

O

Oak leaves, 44, 78
Oasis, 15, 27, 30, 117
October, 12
Oil of roses, 90
Oils, 94, 98
Okra, 53
Old-fashioned scents, 45, 89-98
Onions, 113, 114
Orange
  blossoms, 110
  flowers, 93, 94
  peel, 93, 94
  seeds, 112
Oranges, 11, 44, 96
Orchids, 20, 31
Oregano, 104
Orris root, 93, 94, 96
Owl decorations, 11, 48, 49

La Porte County Library
La Porte, Indiana
Phone 2740

INPUT